Look before you leap?

Research evidence for the
curriculum at Key Stage 2

Look before you leap?

**Research evidence for the
curriculum at Key Stage 2**

Edited by Andrew Pollard

the Tufnell Press

the Tufnell Press,
47 Dalmeny Road,
London, N7 0DY

This collection copyright © 1994, BERA and ASPE
Introduction © *Andrew Pollard*, Chapter 1 © *Jim Campbell and Hilary Emery*, Chapter 2 *Neville Bennett, Mike Summers and Mike Askew*, Chapter 3 *Hilary Burgess, Geoff Southworth and Rosemary Webb*, Chapter 4 © *Pam Sammons, Ann Lewis, Maggie MacLure, Jeni Riley, Neville Bennett and Andrew Pollard*, Chapter 5 © *Ann Lewis and Pam Sammons*

First published January 1994

British Library Cataloguing-in-Publication Data
A catalogue record for this book is
available from the British Library

ISBN 1 872767 12 5

Printed in England by Da Costa Print, London

Contents

Acknowledgements

We would like to acknowledge the support of the National Council's of both the British Educational Research Association and the Association for the Study of Primary Education in initiating and facilitating the work which has led to this publication. Particular support was offered by Caroline Gipps and Wynne Harlen, successive Presidents of BERA, and Jim Campbell, National Chair of ASPE.

A number of people made valuable contributions to our discussions at various points, but were not part of the final writing teams. We would particularly like to acknowledge the input of Christine Stone and participants at the symposium which was convened by the group at the annual conference of the BERA, in Liverpool, in the Autumn of 1993.

The University of the West of England, Bristol, University of Warwick and the London Institute of Eduction provided accommodation and sustainance for our meetings for which we are grateful.

Additionally, we would like to acknowledge the work of Sarah Butler, of the Faculty of Education, University of the West of England, Bristol, who has provided excellent administrative support to the group throughout its work and has been responsible for production of the final, integrated manuscript.

Finally, we thank the Tufnell Press for undertaking very rapid publication of this collection so that it could contribute to public debate.

Andrew Pollard,
Faculty of Education,
University of the West of England, Bristol
January, 1994

CHAPTER ONE

BACK TO SOME DIFFERENT 'BASICS': ISSUES FOR THE NATIONAL CURRICULUM AT KEY STAGE 2

Andrew Pollard

INTRODUCTION

As I write in the Autumn of 1993, there is a major government initiative to promote the movement of social and educational policy 'Back to Basics'. We still suffer, we are told, too much from the influence of the progressive and trendy 1960s. What we need, is more 'commonsense' (Major 1993).

This is challenging advice in all sorts of ways and it can, in particular, be used to introduce some of the issues which are raised in this book. Let us begin by considering three examples of 'commonsense'.

> *Commonsense* suggests that people 'look before they leap'. When they do not, they cannot be quite sure where they will land.
>
> *Commonsense* suggests that people draw on the advice of others with specialist understanding or experience before making important decisions. When they do not, they are likely to make predictable mistakes.
>
> *Commonsense* suggests that people test their beliefs before gambling heavily on them. When they do not, they risk considerable losses.

Such 'basics' are, of course, used by individuals all the time. For instance, they are deployed in domestic decision making, as in Mrs. Thatcher's invocation of the careful, budget-conscious housewife, and in industrial decision making through research and development activities, consultancy and small-scale trialing of new initiatives before major investments.

Sadly, it is true to say that the educational reforms of the late 1980s and early 1990s would have benefited from such commonsense precautions. As it was, education policy moved forward with a bold, but almost blind, decisiveness and on a system-wide scale which, if problems arose, was likely to replicate difficulties across the 25,000 schools of England and Wales and in the experiences of all of their seven million school-aged children.

'Basically', this was not wise.

Indeed, in essence, England and Wales participated in a great experiment which, whilst expected to produce rising educational standards in the long-term, suffered from its insecure grounding in 'commonsense' planning and coordination. Its implementation produced many problems, including curriculum overload, teacher stress, assessment impracticability, management diversion from educational issues and accountability charades. In such a context, the nature and circumstances of the innovation are instructive.

The National Curriculum and its associated assessment procedures were introduced in England by the passage of the Education Reform Act, 1988. This legislation followed a sustained period of criticism of educational provision, particularly deriving from the government and media, and was designed, above all, to raise standards through a restructuring of education for the 1990s. Among many significant features of these reforms was the specification of nine subjects which, with Religious Education, were to structure the basic content of the curriculum at primary school level, and the introduction of a ten level scale of attainment through which pupil achievements could be assessed and recorded throughout their school careers. The schedule for the introduction of such new requirements was rapid and such implementation took place in the context of many other changes, such as the introduction of local management of schools (LMS), the gradual weakening of support structures provided by local education authorities and new requirements for teacher appraisal and for school inspection.

It is commonly agreed that the Education Reform Act, and, indeed, much succeeding legislation, was ideologically driven by various pressure groups which have been associated with the 'New Right' (e.g.: Ball 1989). Certainly the new legislation and structures, can be seen as reflecting the fundamental concern of the New Right with the creation of educational markets through the provision of more information to parental consumers, the weakening of teacher and local authority power and the increase in the accountability of individual schools. However, following the passage of the Educational Reform Act, a great deal of influence was also exerted by educationalists in interpreting the legislation and in influencing its detailed implementation. Formative contributions were made, for example, to the groups which proposed the specific curriculum content for each subject. Such work, of course, reflected a rather different 'professional' ideology which, despite the diversity of specialist contributions, arguably had one underlying purpose—to mediate what was often seen as the 'worse effects' of the legislation and to try to introduce 'positive benefits' from the process of change.

The result of these two major contributions to the structure, content and processes which became incorporated into the National Curriculum was an edifice of considerable scale and complexity but with little coherence. As it was implemented, progressively, through the turn of the decade, the difficulties became increasingly apparent.

This brings us to the present collection.

The papers within this book derive from the work of a task group of fourteen active researchers which met during the 1992/3 academic year to review the acticalities and consequences of attempting to implement the National Curriculum in primary schools, with particular reference to Key Stage 2. The work of the group was initiated by an independent organisation, the British Educational Research Association (BERA), and it was developed with the support of the Association for the Study of Primary Education (ASPE), a major UK association committed to the disinterested study of primary education.

The task group worked under British Educational Research Association's 'standing orders for policy task groups' (May 1992). These standing orders define the purposes of the task groups as:

> to organise the discussion, review and critique of policy research,
>
> to encourage and promote the dissemination of policy research,
>
> to endeavour to provide opportunities for policy makers to be appraised of research findings pertinent to their decisions.

In other words, the task group did indeed set out to go 'back to basics', but this was interpreted in terms of clarifying those findings and issues suggested by educational research which might contribute to the future deliberations of the government and other groups engaged in policy formation regarding the primary school curriculum. The aims of the group were thus entirely constructive, though they were not uncritical. Indeed, when the task group began this work in the Autumn of 1992, several members of the group had published analyses which doubted the continuation of the National Curriculum in the form in which it then existed.

In the circumstances of late 1992, our strategy was to focus on what we saw as major fundamental issues as a means of generating a better holistic understanding of the curriculum at Key Stage 2. This, we believed, would provide a platform for any future review which might arise. Of course, at that time we did not anticipate the speed with which an actual review would take place following the continuous revelation of difficulties in implementation, the closure of the National Curriculum Council (NCC) and School Examinations and Assessment Council (SEAC) and the Secretary of State's decision to appoint Sir Ron Dearing to lead the new School Curriculum and Assessment Authority (SCAA).

It is important then to emphasise the main aims of the task group. It has attempted to review and synthesise some of the most important findings and analyses which derive from research of recent years and which have a bearing on the National Curriculum at Key Stage 2. It has not sought to engage directly with all the details of policy implementation and change. Rather, it has regarded its role as reviewing research evidence and offered this as a contribution to the work of those who do have the responsibility to engage in detailed policy review. Indeed, first drafts of the papers in this collection were provided for SCAA and Sir Ron Dearing in the Autumn of 1993.

THE PAPERS: AN EXECUTIVE SUMMARY

In this section, the key arguments of each of the papers are summarised. This provides a quick overview of the contents of the papers, but readers should beware. The full papers contain important information, evidence, arguments and qualifications which are not always conveyed in the executive summary.

Curriculum policy

The first paper, by Jim Campbell and Hilary Emery, draws attention to the limitations which exist in the provision of a curriculum which is both broad and balanced. Amongst the evidence and arguments which are deployed are the following:

Half of teaching time in Key Stage 2 classrooms is spent on the 'basics' of English and mathematics because of high professional and parental priority and the pressure of assessment requirements. This reflects continuities with the past and is unlikely to change. Given the time needed for other non–curricular activities, only 40% of time is available for the other eight non–basic subjects. This is inadequate for worthwhile learning.

Provision of a broad and balanced curriculum could only be achieved by reducing, or integrating, some of the time currently spent on separate teaching of English and maths.

Teachers' knowledge

In the second paper of the collection, Neville Bennett, Mike Summers and Mike Askew focus on teachers and on the knowledge which they need of both subject matter and of how to teach it to children. From the evidence which they review, the situation is revealed to be very challenging indeed, particularly given recent decisions to change the nature of initial teacher training:

Primary teachers very often lack the subject knowledge and associated teaching knowledge necessary to implement the National Curriculum effectively. In initial training, PGCE courses are too short to provide this knowledge. The proposed decrease in length of undergraduate teaching from four to three years with coverage of more subjects may put greater strain on student's acquisition of in–depth subject knowledge. In both cases, school–based training is likely to compound the problem.

Increased specialist teaching has its attractions, but apart from the challenge posed to the prevailing culture of the primary school, begs the question of whether the profession can attract specialists, especially in mathematics and science. Also, the sizes of many primary schools are such that the scope for specialist staffing is limited.

Coherent, long–term programmes of induction and in–service training could be effective but present provision is fragmented. Such continuous professional development should be informed by broad–based competencies.

Any revisions of the National Curriculum should reflect an analysis of subject and pedagogic knowledge which are required.

Whole school issues

Hilary Burgess, Geoff Southworth and Rosemary Webb consider whole school planning. They discuss recent research on school culture and the concept of 'whole school', the implications for curriculum planning and the roles and responsibilities of teachers and headteachers. As they put it:

The organisational context in which teachers work and in which the curriculum is implemented is of great significance and there is evidence of the effectiveness of whole school planning. However, there are still some tensions between previous practices in primary schools, which offered teachers large degrees of autonomy, and the present need for whole–school curriculum planning and collaboration.

The content and processes of whole school planning for the National Curriculum are relatively new to many teachers. The nature and quality of headteachers' management and leadership have been vital given the rapidity and scale of change and the range of external pressures on teachers. However, many headteachers have found that management responsibilities are compromising their capacity to provide curriculum leadership. Deputy headteachers also often face very heavy workloads and diverse responsibilities for both a class and for whole school issues.

Most teachers have curriculum subject co–ordination responsibilities, often for more than one subject. However, these roles often create large expectations with few available resources or opportunities to discharge them.

Effective whole school planning is facilitated by shared institutional values, appropriate organisational structures, adequate resources and leadership. More school–based and off–site INSET support is needed.

Teaching and learning processes

The fourth paper takes on a wide–ranging set of interconnected issues and a considerable number of research findings are reviewed by Pam Sammons, Ann Lewis, Maggie MacLure, Jeni Riley, Neville Bennett and Andrew Pollard. In terms of specific themes, the paper considers classroom organisation, pupil learning, language and learning, pupils' experiences, assessment, resources and entitlements. In so doing, the paper reveals the complexity of classroom processes and the need for professional judgement in reaching pedagogic and curricular decisions on appropriateness. Amongst the major points which are made are:

In public discussion of education, this topic of teaching and learning processes has often not received the quality of attention which it deserves. It is complex but of enormous significance.

Teacher stress, workloads and curriculum over–specification are beginning to impact adversely on learning processes.

Children are active participants in their learning and language is the central medium of this learning. Teachers, and curriculum policy-makers, need to understand the role of adults in extending pupil understanding through discussion, instruction and questioning. Teachers need to have a repertoire of teaching strategies on which to draw, as appropriate for their specific aims.

Pupil perceptions and experiences in school have not changed a great deal since the introduction of the National Curriculum. In particular, they remain very aware of teacher power.

Formative assessment continues to offer the potential of enhancing teaching and learning processes and the constructive involvement of parents. Evidence suggests that Standard Assessment Tasks are unreliable and of limited value. The issues of negative labelling and stereotyping in Teacher Assessment need to be kept under review.

Children with special needs

The final paper in the collection, by Ann Lewis and Pam Sammons, focuses on the impact of the National Curriculum on primary school children with special educational needs. The efficacy of the National Curriculum for children with special needs has remained an important litmus test of the wider effectiveness and appropriateness of that curriculum. Curricular provision for children with special needs must be seen in the wider context of market–oriented aspects of the 1988 and 1993 Education Acts, notably the finance of education, open enrolment and 'opting out'. This broader picture raises concerns about the educational experiences of many children with special needs.

Lewis and Sammons review the available evidence about curricular provision for children with special needs:

These pupils comprise a large minority of the school population, about one child in five. However the proportion of children with statements of special needs is much smaller and varies widely between local education authorities. This is significant because the statement is intended to provide a guarantee of additional resources to meet the child's needs.

The effect of the 1993 Education Act and associated draft Code of Practice is likely to be a marked reduction in the proportion of children with statements. This will be in the context of a diminishing pool of local and school–based expertise on special needs, reduced LEA powers of coordination and an increased proportion of children excluded from schools.

The development of greater expertise in special needs provision in mainstream schools is a major priority. Training needs to be aimed both at classroom teachers and, importantly given the responsibilities of special needs coordinators proposed in the draft Code of Practice, leaders in mainstream special needs provision.

Differentiation of teaching methods and/or curricular content have been fostered as ways of enhancing the inclusivity of mainstream curricula. The difficulties in implementing these strategies reflect the low awareness of special needs concerns within the existing National Curriculum structure and have serious resource implications.

Assessment procedures must be capable of recognising the achievements and progress of children with special needs. Value–added approaches are likely to be important in encouraging schools to demonstrate gains in learning, not merely end scores.

The curriculum continuity provided by the National Curriculum supports the quality of multi–professional and cross–sector links for children with special needs.

SOME 'BASIC' CONCLUSIONS

Overall, members of the British Educational Research Association/Association for the Study of Primary Education Policy Task Group on Primary Education have documented the immense complexity of the relationships between teaching, learning, curriculum and assessment in meeting the needs of all children within the present structures of school, LEA and central government provision.

An important point to emphasise is that there certainly is strong support among teachers and parents for the principle of having a national curriculum. Indeed, in introducing such a curriculum for England and Wales, the Education Reform Act 1988 has contributed to educational provision in a very significant way indeed. However, as we have seen in the executive summaries above and as is spelt out in the full papers, there are a great many specific points of both principle and implementation which should have been considered in the construction of the

National Curriculum and certainly need to be considered in its continuing evaluation and review.

In concluding this introduction to the collection, I will draw out two more generalised 'basics' to which the task group would certainly urge the government to 'return'.

First, is the need for a flexible and enabling curriculum framework. The range and complexity of the educational issues involved in pupil learning clearly suggests that, whilst national frameworks for curriculum, assessment, resourcing and professional development are important to ensure entitlement and to develop provision, over–specification within such frameworks of subject content and study time will lead to failure. National education policies need to be constructed in such a way that it is possible to adapt them to meet local circumstances and the specific needs of pupils and teachers.

Second, is the development of greater trust, respect and partnership between the government and teachers. On this issue, the government and others must genuinely recognise and build on the vital role of skilled, knowledgeable and committed teachers in using professional judgement and taking contextually appropriate action in providing for the children in their care.

One could say that these are basic, 'commonsense' principles—and one might hope that they will be spared the accusation of being 'trendy', 'progressive' or redolent of the 1960s. Now, no less than thirty years later, there is a greater need than ever to build new, stable and constructive partnerships in education. At the same time though, as the papers in this collection show, there are many unresolved issues and difficulties to be surmounted. As educational researchers specialising in primary education we can but offer work of the sort contained in this book as one contribution to the debates and developments of the future.

CHAPTER TWO

CURRICULUM POLICY FOR KEY STAGE 2: POSSIBILITIES, CONTRADICTIONS AND CONSTRAINTS

Jim Campbell and Hilary Emery

INTRODUCTION

Our purpose in this paper is a threefold one. First, to show that the policy for the primary curriculum, as it was conceived and has emerged over the period since 1987, assumed a curriculum model embodying ambitiously designed and much-needed improvement to curriculum practice in primary schools in England and Wales generally. Second, the successful implementation of the main policy objective—the broad and balanced curriculum—was undermined by mistaken assumptions about time available for curriculum delivery, historical and cultural influences on curriculum priorities held by teachers, and by the contradictions in government policy on assessment, recording and reporting. All these have created limits to the reform process. Third, some policy issues associated with the attempt to implement the broad and balanced curriculum in primary schools are explored.

Two cautions are necessary. The first is obvious. In 1993 the national curriculum was not fully in place in its statutory form in any school at either Key Stage 1 or Key Stage 2. At Key Stage 1, the last three subjects—Art, P.E. and Music— applied in statutory form only in 1992–93. At Key Stage 2, all nine (or ten in Wales) subjects were to apply to all pupils in 1995–1996 at the earliest, before the revisions associated with the Dearing review's interim report (Dearing 1993). We would also stress the tentativeness of the available research evidence about implementation at Key Stage 2 since nearly all evidence refers to Key Stage 1 only.

The second introductory point is more difficult to make briefly. Under the imposed reforms of the 1988 Act there has been a tendency among educationists to invent a 'Golden Age' of primary education in the past, whose destruction has been brought about by the reform process. The image of this Golden Age was derived from the Plowden Report (CACE 1967) in which rounded pictures were presented of good practice in a part of the report (para. 277ff) where 'composite' schools were seen through the eyes of an 'imaginary visitor', based upon a child-centred approach to teaching and learning. The image offered was concrete, detailed and suffused with light and joy, showing a school world of emotional security and wellbeing for pupils, combined with a range of artistic and cultural activities apparently unconstrained by time, or the pupils' age, or intellectual shortcomings among staff or pupils. On this reading of the history of postwar primary education, children's spontaneity, creativity and curiosity were being killed off in the name of curriculum reform.

As a picture of curriculum practice it was a fiction. The evidence from HMI surveys (e.g. DES 1978b, 1982, 1985b) and research (e.g. Alexander 1984, 1992; Bennett 1976; Bennett *et al.* 1980; Galton and Simon 1980; Barker–Lunn 1982, 1984; Bealing 1972) about curriculum practice and pedagogy in primary schools in the twenty–odd years before the Education Reform Act revealed not a golden, so much as a rather leaden, age. In many cases, HMI identified a narrow curriculum, emphasising literacy and numeracy through repetitive exercises (DES 1978b, 1989a, 1989b, 1990a); despite encouragement, work in Science was patchy and haphazard; standards in the social subjects were lower than might be expected; pedagogy was often characterised by an undifferentiated focus on the pupils in the middle levels of attainment within a class, and expectations of the able children were undemanding. Continuity and progression in curriculum experience had remained elusive and assessment and record–keeping, other than in the basic skills of reading and number, were rarely systematic. Despite political assertions blaming Plowdenesque progressivism for much of our supposed decline in educational standards, generally progressive practice, however defined, was an approach used by a minority of teachers.

If this general practice is to be criticised, we would argue that the fault lay not with teachers but with the absence of anything approaching a public policy for the primary curriculum before 1988 (see Campbell 1989). Primary teachers, as much as anyone else, were the victims of this policy vacuum and not its creators.

ISSUES, EVIDENCE AND CONSEQUENCES

The Policy Framework post–1988

What the 1988 Act introduced was a policy framework for the curriculum that had been previously lacking in primary education. The framework had five features of especial interest here.

First, there was the concept of entitlement. Articulated most clearly in the House of Commons 3rd Report (House of Commons 1986), a national curriculum would provide a legal framework of common entitlement for children that would remove the inconsistencies of curricular provision, (see Richards 1982), which had arisen arbitrarily from class teacher autonomy. For the first time since 1944 pupils and parents would be able to know what the school should provide in curriculum terms, as would the school staff and governors. In effect, the notion of entitlement promised greater equality, or at least similarity, of curricular experience for children.

Second, and linked to the concept of entitlement, was the promise of breadth and balance. A statutory curriculum in which all foundation subjects, not just the core, would be allocated reasonable amounts of time and emphasis, seemed to offer a once–and–for–all opportunity to destroy the elementary approach to curriculum with its narrow concentration on basic skills. The 1988 Education Act required a 'balanced and broadly based' curriculum, and the DES Circular 5/89 (DES 1989c) emphasised breadth and balance (p. 17) requiring, from August 1989, that each of the core and foundation subjects should be allocated 'reasonable' time for worthwhile study.

Third, included in the legal definition of the curriculum was a set of assessment arrangements which would require a radical rethinking not merely of assessment but also of teaching itself. The TGAT report (DES 1988) was sold to the profession by its emphasis on the formative purposes of assessment. Before 1988 most assessment in primary schools had employed narrowly focused tests of reading comprehension and number, and tests of intelligence, predominantly at the end of the infant and junior stages, (see Gipps 1988, 1990). Under the TGAT proposals the emphasis would shift to continuous teacher assessment. This would be based on observations and discussion of children's learning and its outcomes, involving diagnosing individual pupils' needs and using this evidence for planning the next steps in learning.

There was evident tension between assessment requirements that teachers accepted as valid and over–complex presentation of how these should be developed from Key Stage 1. Shorrocks (1991, p. 232) cites the three SEAC Guides to Teacher Assessment, Packs A, B and C, which, despite containing useful, important material on assessment, were poorly received. This may have been partly caused by an apparent lack of awareness of demands on schools in INSET time. Pack B of the Guides (SEAC 1989) set unrealistic expectations of a programme of school development sessions on assessment over a term. Generally, paperwork from SEAC has been perceived as becoming increasingly complex and extensive.

At Key Stage 1 tension was caused by inconsistencies between interpretation of SoA between different agencies and schools. This was heightened because of insufficient time for agreement trialing leading to a sense of threat, of being overwhelmed and deskilled (Shorrocks 1991). Such tensions were restricting the potential in the assessment arrangement for substantial teacher development.

Moves at Key Stage 1 to save teacher time as a result of the evaluations in 1989 (NFER 1989, p. 63, and Shorrocks 1991, p. 61) led to the loss of some of the process aspects of assessment in Mathematics and Science. Those were the ones most closely tied to normal classroom practice, e.g. activity based, small group work approach to assessment. Despite all these technical and communication problems, the potential for teacher development through new forms of assessment was considerable.

Fourth, it was a modernising curriculum. It was not merely that Science was included in the core but that the kind of Science involved acknowledged advances in Physics, Biology and Chemistry; Technology, including Information Technology, was in the foundation; Mathematics included the handling of data, and most other subjects called for Information Technology applications. English called for literature that was global. The national curriculum was, in effect, an attempt to haul the primary curriculum towards a state of knowledge and information processing relevant to the latter decade of the 20th Century.

Finally, there was the relationship of the curriculum to standards. Primary education in England and Wales had been characterised by relatively low standards, especially in relation to children judged to be able (DES 1978b, DES 1990c, Alexander *et al.* 1992). The common and possibly facile explanation for this state of affairs was that teacher expectations were too low, especially in inner cities and other areas of poverty. This was facile because it left local authority housing policies out of the analysis. These tended to cluster pupils who had problems in particular schools, with the consequence that it was hard to avoid having low expectations confirmed.

A series of important observational studies at Exeter University (Bennett *et al.* 1984, Bennett and Dunne 1992, Bennett 1991, 1992), provided demonstration of poor match between tasks set by teachers and pupil capacities (or, to be precise, sometimes poor teacher explanation of the task) and might lend force to the argument that the national curriculum to raise standards, specifically by raising expectations of able children through the explicitly differentiated levels in which the attainment targets were specified. Able children at the end of Key Stage 1 would be operating at Levels 3 or 4, and at the end of Key Stage 2 at Levels 5 or 6. In addition, standards would be raised simply by virtue of teaching being planned, delivered and assessed according to systematic programmes of study and set attainment targets right across the nine subject areas. Standards would no longer be defined narrowly by reference to standards in English and Mathematics.

Thus the promotion of the national curriculum model held out the ambitious promise of a transformation of curriculum practice in primary schools, irrespective of other, political, motivations for its introduction.

The Curriculum Model and the Workplace Culture

There are problems with the curriculum model itself (see Kelly 1990 for example), but we wish first to explore the relationship between policy on the primary curriculum, and the workplace culture of primary schools. We use the term 'workplace culture' rather loosely, following Evetts (1990), to mean the generally accepted practice or methods of doing the job and their underlying values. Despite the absurdity of generalising about 19,000–odd schools, we wish to draw attention to five features that may affect policy implementation. Three are adapted from Evetts (1990) and are:

i)   Small size, and therefore close, regular daily contact between all teachers in an organisation fairly well insulated from others, which does not tolerate too much conflict.

ii) Conceptions of the job as largely generalist and welfare in orientation, with low levels of perceived specialist competencies or professionality.

iii) Gender imbalance, with its implied heavy burden of domestic work outside school for most teachers.

To these three we would want to add two attitudinal characteristics: a high cultural premium on demonstrated conscientious effort (Campbell *et al.* 1991), and high levels of deference to perceived educational authority (Alexander 1992). Until recently these two attitudes were revealed in a readiness to adopt any reforms labelled as "good practice" by LEA inspectors and advisers, or they were transformed into a cynical acceptance of reforms as the latest bandwagon. You had to jump onto it but you could mime playing the instruments.

There are three preliminary points about our concentration on the workplace culture. First, the workplace culture is the medium through which all educational reforms must pass, but little attention has been directed to it in respect of the current reforms. Secondly, because of its value system, the culture is likely to allocate differential salience in teachers' eyes to different parts of the policy initiative. Third, the OFSTED report (OFSTED 1993b) argued that the Alexander, Rose and Woodhead paper (Alexander *et al.* 1992) had challenged the primary school culture. Certainly the paper posed challenges to the primary school rhetoric, and that the challenge was overdue, but it would be wrong to underestimate the strength of resistance to change in workplace cultures.

The Broad and Balanced Curriculum

We can consider the broad and balanced curriculum mainly in terms of the time allocated to particular subjects, though we accept that the quality of learning activities within the time is a more fundamental research issue (see Alexander *et al.* 1992). Despite exceptions, the school culture before 1988 had emphasised an elementary school ideology in curriculum matters, with very large proportions of time allocated to the two basic subjects of English and Mathematics. Bassey (1977), the DES Primary Survey (DES 1978b), the Bennett *et al.* (1980) study of open plan schools, Galton and Simon's (1980) ORACLE study, the Primary Staffing Survey (DES 1987a), Tizard *et al.* (1988), Alexander's (1992) Leeds study, all showed, despite technical difficulties in agreeing how to allocate proportions of time to given subjects, that about half the timetabled time was given over to these two subjects, leaving relatively small amounts of time available for everything else. Data (Campbell and Neill forthcoming) on Key Stage 1 and Key Stage 2 in 1991/1992 show proportions of time allocated to Maths and English combined, eerily identical to the proportion shown for these two subjects in the

Primary Staffing Survey of 1987. The Primary Staffing survey gave a spuriously accurate 49.1%, while Campbell & Neill showed, equally spuriously, 49% (Key Stage 2) and 51% (Key Stage 1). The findings of all the studies cited above are summarised in tabular form in Appendix I.

The findings are not surprising, and indeed Meyer, Kamens and Benavot (1992) demonstrate in their book, School Knowledge for the Masses, that there has been an elementary model of the curriculum, relatively homogeneous across cultures in the first 80 years of this century, representing a kind of Chomskian deep structure shared by all primary curricula, framed by global forces. They show that, irrespective of culture, national politics, state of economic development or geography, official primary curricula devote about a third of the time to the national language, about one sixth to Mathematics (i.e. together = 50% of the time); a set of other subjects—Science, Social Studies, Arts and Physical Education—get about one tenth each, with Moral/Religious Education and other matters getting the other tenth. As Meyer summarises these findings:

> 'The stylized character of the overall outline of the curriculum is striking.
> Put simply, curricular categories, and even allocations of time to these
> categories, conform to a standard world outline', (p. 166).

Thus the evidence, both here and globally, indicates how ambitious the national curriculum model in England and Wales was. Whether consciously or not, it had to break the mould of the historical/global elementary emphasis in the primary curriculum by moving towards a reduction of the time for two basic subjects because Science was incorporated into the 50% core. The time freed up in this way would be available to the reintroduced subjects of History and Geography and the new subject of Technology, together with the ambiguously framed subjects of Art, P.E. and Music, the statutory requirement to teach R.E. and other teaching. There is support for the above argument in the fact that advice from the National Curriculum Council on planning the Key Stage 2 curriculum (NCC 1993a) gave illustrative examples in which only 37% and 41% of time was to be spent on the two basic subjects.

Some Limitations on Reform

This ambitious policy has run into three powerful obstacles, not through primary teachers' subversion, which has been lacking, but at the level of the workplace culture. The first obstacle was structural in that policy assumptions about the time available for teaching were mistaken. The assumptions are shown in Appendix II, which shows the notional proportions of time allocated to each subject given as guidance to the subject working groups. One problem with this is 'evaporated time', (ILEA 1988). Evaporated time is time technically available for teaching but having to be used for activities such as transition (moving pupils from one place to another) and supervision. This has been known to characterise working practices in primary schools from the research literature, (see Gump 1976; Bennett *et al.* 1980). According to Campbell & Neill (1992), just under 10% of the teaching time at Key Stage 1 in the week was taken up in transition and supervision, so that there was less time available for teaching than was assumed by the national curriculum working groups, and it amounted to more than the equivalent of one whole national curriculum subject.

But, more importantly, there are two cultural pressures on teachers to retain their heavy time emphasis on the two basic subjects. First, the elementary tradition continues to operate as a powerful historical force upon teachers' perceptions of curricular priorities, giving the teaching of Reading and the teaching of basic number extremely high salience in the school culture, especially at Key Stage 1 where parental pressure provides contemporary reinforcement.

Secondly, and ironically, another arm of government policy, namely that on end–of–Key–Stage 2 testing, assessment, recording, reporting and publication of results, runs directly counter to, and undermines, the policy on delivering the broad and balanced curriculum. The policy decision has been to concentrate the end–of–Key–Stage 2 testing upon the three core subjects (including the basics in Mathematics and English) and to make the assessment arrangements what the Americans call 'high stakes' (Madaus, quoted in Gipps 1990) in the sense that the school's reputation in its community, and even a part of its funding base, might depend upon the results. As Gipps (1990) shows, this was bound to wash back into the curriculum and, we would argue, into the allocation of curriculum time to the core.

Thus, an unholy Trinity of a structural shortage of curriculum time, the historical influence of the elementary ideology, and governmental policy on testing and publication of results reinforces continuing high salience in the school culture at Key Stage 2 for the basic subjects, with consequently inadequate time for the non–basic subjects, especially History and Geography and R.E. according to the evidence (Campbell and Neill 1992, OFSTED 1993b). Against this Trinity the policy for the delivery of a broad and balanced curriculum is weak, with very low salience. It means that the broad and balanced curriculum has not been, and probably cannot be, delivered, despite conscientious attempts to do so. It also helps explain some of the high teacher stress levels reported.

Campbell and Neill (1990, 1992) show that the three core subjects were taking, on average, at least half the timetabled time and that, at the very most, about 15 minutes a day were left for each of the other foundation subjects and R.E. Most of these subjects at Key Stage 1 are practical, time–consuming activities, e.g. Art, P.E., Music, Technology, and 15 minutes per day (75 minutes a week) seemed inadequate for worthwhile treatment. Campbell & Neill point out that, for technical reasons concerning how time was recorded, the figure of 15 minutes a day per subject is almost certainly an overstatement. The core was squeezing out the other parts of the basic curriculum at Key stages 1 and 2. This view was supported by Muschamp *et al.* (1992).

This point can be examined in greater detail from new data from a longitudinal study of Key Stage 1 teachers being carried out at Warwick University between 1990–1993, (see Campbell and Neill 1990, 1992 for methods and sampling). Tables 1 and 2 show the 1992 data. One hundred and five teachers were asked to indicate to which of the core and foundation subjects and R.E. they thought they had been able to devote adequate time in their class in 1992. They were able to indicate all ten subjects, or none, or as many as reflected their perception. Ninety-seven teachers replied, so that if they all thought that all the subjects had received adequate time there would have been 970 responses; if they thought that none of the subjects had adequate time there would have been no responses. As can be seen from Table 1, there were 477 responses, suggesting that the teachers overall saw only about half of the curriculum as having had adequate time devoted to it.

Table 1   *Perceived adequacy of time devoted to subjects in Key Stage 1 teachers' classes 1992 (n = 97)*

Subject	(a) No. of Responses	(a) % of Responses	(c) % of Teachers
English	79	6.6	81.4
Mathematics	74	15.5	76.3
Science	63	13.2	64.9
P.E.	58	12.2	59.8
Art	49	10.3	50.5
Technology	34	7.1	35.1
R.E.	34	7.1	35.1
Music	31	6.5	32.0
Geography	28	5.9	28.9
History	27	5.7	27.8
TOTAL	477	100.0	n.a

More detailed examination of Column (c) in Table 1 reveals the teachers' perceptions about individual subjects. In this column the figures are the percentage of teachers thinking that the particular subject had adequate time devoted to it in the current school year.

The differences in perceptions about different subjects are quite striking, given that all subjects were expected to have 'reasonable' time given to them. Teacher perceptions of what is adequate are not a definitive measure, of course, but their views are most important since they are the people responsible for the process of delivery.

We can treat teachers' views on adequacy in two ways, strictly and generously. On a strict view we might say that where less than two thirds of the teachers thought a subject had adequate time, there is a *prima facie* case for saying that there is a problem. On the generous treatment we might say that, where less than half the teachers thought a subject has had adequate time, there is a problem. On the first assumption, only Mathematics and English, in the view of these teachers, had adequate time in 1992; on the second assumption, Science, P.E. and Art had also had adequate time. On either assumption the same five of the ten subjects were seen as having had inadequate time. These were Technology, R.E., Music, and especially Geography and History. The latter two subjects came bottom of the pile with fewer than three teachers in ten thinking that the time devoted to them was adequate.

Campbell & Neill were able to set Table 1 against actual time given to the subjects by the same teachers in ten weeks over the last half of Spring and first half of Summer terms in 1992. This is given in Table 2.

Table 2   *Teaching Time by Curriculum Subjects*

Subject	(a) Hours per week	(b) % of total time	(c) % of sum of column (a)
English	10.8	60	29
Mathematics	6.7	34	18
Science	3.5	19	9
Art	3.3	18	9
Technology	2.6	14	7
P.E.	1.3	7	4
Geography	0.9	5	2
History	0.9	5	2
R.E.	0.5	3	2
Music	0.5	3	1
SATs	2.5	14	7
Teacher Assessment	1.7	9	5
Other Teaching	1.1	6	3
Total time spent teaching	18.0	n.a.	100
Sum of individual subjects	37.5		

Two findings from Table 2 are worth particular comment. There is a highly significant match (Kendall Rank Correlation $p<.001$) between the order of subjects in this table and that in Table 1 above. If we exclude Technology, the 'top' five subjects are identical and in almost identical order. Using the generous definition (viz., that more than 50% of teachers thought the time was adequate) of adequacy above, our evidence is that the teachers perceived English, Mathematics, Science,

Art and P.E. as having adequate time given to them and that they had actually given most time to them. The teachers perceived Geography, History, R.E., Music and Technology as having had inadequate time and, except for Technology, gave the least time to them. The relatively high position of Technology in Table 2 and its low position in Table 1 might be explained by the fact that it normally requires time–consuming, practical investigations, often using computers, and the time recorded, though relatively large, is still seen as inadequate. It should be remembered that in 1992 the statutory orders applied in the core subjects and in History, Geography and Technology, but not in Art, P.E. and Music.

Although not every subject needs the same amount of time for worthwhile delivery, we would argue that, when teachers' perceptions of inadequacy matched a record of relatively low time actually spent, it is very strong evidence that the balanced and broadly based curriculum was not being delivered.

Second, there was a heavy concentration upon the core subjects. There are two ways of calculating this time. The simple one is to note what proportion of the 18 hours given over to teaching included each of the core subjects. This measure gives the proportion of the teaching week during which a classroom visitor would find a subject being taught. This is given in Column (b) of Table 2, which shows that 60%, 34% and 19% of total time included English, Mathematics and Science respectively. Thus English work was occurring during nearly two–thirds of the teaching week. The percentages exceed 100 because teachers often taught two or more subjects simultaneously. The more complex analysis reflects this simultaneous teaching. We can take the sum of time spent on the different subjects, (viz. 37.5 hours), and express the time spent on each as a percentage of this sum. This is done in Column (c) using rounded percentages, and is a better guide to time spent by pupils as a proportion of teaching time in the week, assuming that when several subjects are being taught at the same time pupils are fairly evenly distributed between them. On this analysis, 56% of teaching time was given over to the core, only 30% was given over to the other foundation subjects, R.E. and other subjects, and 12% was given over to Teacher Assessment and SATs. Since all SAT–time and most Teacher Assessment was focused on the core subjects, the 30% figure for the non–core proportion is unlikely to be an underestimate. More time was devoted in the data collection period to SATs and Teacher Assessment, but the figures in Appendix I show the data from across the whole school year, with 51% spent on the two basic subjects and 39% on all others. Irrespective of which analysis is used, these findings show the core to be dominating the curriculum and that, for this reason, the other foundation subjects and R.E. were being squeezed out.

Data (Campbell and Neill forthcoming) of time spent by Key Stage 2 teachers in 1992 is similar, with all non–core subjects taking up only 34% of time.

Basic Curriculum and Basic Assessment?

There is a reinforcing contradiction between the broad and balanced curriculum espoused in the ERA, and DFE regulations for assessment, recording and reporting. The emphasis on the basics is reflected in Circular 14/92 (DFE 1992) where the reporting requirements at the end of Key Stages 1 and 2 ask for subject and AT levels for the core subjects; subject levels for History and Geography; subject and profile component levels for Technology, but only narrative commentaries for Art, Music and P.E. are required.

This emphasis on basics is reinforced in the planned provision of comparative data at the end of Key Stage 2 to parents on other pupils from the school, and national results. As well as aggregated data on levels in all national curriculum subjects statutorily assessed, the reading, writing and spelling attainment targets and the number attainment target from Mathematics (para. 13, p. 10) must be included separately for comparative purposes.

The trialing of external marking of the Key Stage 2 tests can be seen as either a move to improve manageability or to take control away from the schools (SEAC 1993). Whichever the reason, it is likely to cause deskilling and reduced emphasis on the formative purposes of assessment. Ironically, as at Key Stage 3, the timing of the assessment process was inappropriate in terms of transfer arrangements between schools from Key Stage 2 to Key Stage 3, or in terms of subject selection for Key Stage 4 by Key Stage 3 pupils, both of which occur during the late Autumn and early Spring of the year. If we are to move to really useful assessment that affects the educational process and impacts on manageability, the timing is crucial and needs revision. Some Key Stage 2 schools, in agreement with their Key Stage 3 colleagues, intend to continue use of standardised tests in the Autumn term as the data provided were deemed necessary for setting/grouping, etc. (Emery *et al.* 1993).

The requirement to keep evidence of assessment has caused an enormous burden on teachers. Despite guidance materials (e.g., SEAC Key Stage 1 and 3 School Assessment Folders and the 1992 Assessment Orders from DFE), NFER's research at Key Stage 3 found many heads of department were unclear about expectations, and practice varied widely (NFER and Brunel 1992, p. 21) They found that there was no evidence of consistent requirements of amounts of evidence necessary to attain a SoA or level in the process attainment targets (Ma1 and Sc1) (ibid. p. 34), and suggested that schools needed to institute systematic monitoring by senior management of teacher assessment.

Gipps (1992a) noted the need for teachers actively to engage in researching their practice of teaching and assessing in order to develop their expertise and find effective and manageable approaches. Her position has been criticised on the grounds that it ignores the reality of workloads and political expectations, and assumes the appropriateness and usefulness of the assessment system itself

(Torrance 1992). Thus, although there is uncertainty arising from the need to balance workload against the benefits of formative assessment, the concentration of the publicly reported test results continues to reinforce the professional practice of emphasising the basics (or possibly the core).

DISCUSSION

Some Gains

None of the foregoing is to assert that there have not been significant gains over previous practice. The most obvious is the allocation of substantially increased time to Science. After decades of voluntary curriculum development in Science failed to ensure systematic Science teaching in primary schools, statutory imposition, supported by earmarked funding for INSET, led to significant increase in the amount of time devoted to the subject. This is an uncomfortable lesson for the democratic curriculum developer. And there is the advantage of the specified content in History and Geography, and the growing skills of teachers in formative assessment (OFSTED 1993b). Nevertheless, the broad and balanced curriculum, or at least the balanced curriculum with reasonable time devoted to all subjects, cannot be delivered, for the reasons advanced above.

The Defects of the Current Proposals for Review

It follows that current policy readjustments (Patten 1993, Dearing 1993) to create a slimmed–down version of the curriculum will be largely unsuccessful since they address only the first of the three obstacles—viz. the shortage of time in the school week—by reducing the curriculum overload. They do little to affect the historical influence, and the policy contradiction of the assessment arrangements remains in force. Attempts to increase the school day, or week, or year, would not, in themselves, ameliorate the problem since there could be little prospect of teachers devoting any extra time thus gained to subjects other than the testable core. Indeed, given the evidence (Campbell *et al.* 1991, NCC 1992d) that teachers at Key Stage 1 believed that time to hear children read was suffering, it might be predicted that all extra time would be directed to Language. Thus there is a built–in source of permanent failure of the policy on the broad and balanced curriculum, with a fundamental contradiction at the heart of government policy, and unless policy on assessment at Key Stages 1 and 2 is changed—most improbable considering the political priority given to it—the statutory entitlement to a broad and balanced curriculum cannot be realised.

Two Abandoned Initiatives

There were two policy initiatives that would have strengthened the broad and balanced push. One was the intention expressed in the first Consultation Document from the DES (1987b) on the national curriculum to specify time allocations or proportions for each subject, as is often done in other national curricula. This would have given some public protection to the non–core subjects but, ironically, it was seen by the educational establishment as a mechanistic top–down approach to curriculum planning, and would presumably require changes to the 1988 Act if it were to be introduced. But the proposal from the interim review (Dearing 1993) to issue guidance about time allocations is potentially an important development, provided that protection for the non–basics is its prime objective.

The other initiative was to focus the reporting and publication of end–of–Key–Stage testing on all subjects, not just the core, as TGAT proposed initially. But this is not now a realistic option politically or professionally, given the implications for workload.

The Potential for School Policies on Homework
Consideration of the allocation of curriculum time generates a tangential issue—whether, at Key Stage 2 in particular, we ought to stop thinking about pupil time on the curriculum as synonymous with the timetabled school day and to examine the potential of more systematic approaches to homework as a way of increasing curriculum time. Since the very term "homework" may cause concern let us add that we mean an extension of the kind of parental involvement and partnership schemes developed mostly at Key Stage 1 for Reading, which might reduce the excessive school time currently devoted to English. As can be seen from Appendices I and II, it is reduction in time for English that has been assumed in the policy guidance on time allocation, with a reduction from the 30% in practice to 20% in the policy assumptions.

Towards an Unbalanced Curriculum?
It is worth asking whether the policy concept of the balanced curriculum should be differently formulated for Key Stage 1 and Key Stage 2. The notional guidance given to the working groups indicated similar proportions of time for Mathematics and English, for example, for both Key Stages. Given the significance of the teaching of reading and early number work at Key Stage 1, the policy framework is, to say the least, problematic. Why not have an 'unbalanced' curriculum at Key Stage 1, concentrating quite legitimately on the core subjects of Mathematics, English and Science, with choice given to schools about what else to include?

Implications for the Revision of the Key Stage 2 Curriculum
Finally, the Secretary of State's intention (Patten 1993) to have 'curriculum evolution' over a five–year period, and its initiation by Dearing review (Dearing 1993), is problematic for four reasons.

First, if it is conducted serially, i.e., subject by subject, the whole curriculum balance may remain unaddressed, not least because the order of the subjects revised creates problems for what comes last from what has been revised first.

Second, it runs the risk of reducing the credibility of the curriculum policy itself, especially amongst a profession which is largely deferential to authority. You can impose changes upon such teachers fairly effectively (despite what Fullan (1991) says) initially, but with each succeeding change credibility is damaged. Black (1993) thought this had happened to Science teachers at the first revision of Science. Thus, the Dearing moratorium on further revision to existing orders is to be supported. Nonetheless, and this is deliberately put in a caricatured form, teachers have worked hard, under considerable stress, to implement the existing curriculum as well as they can, only to feel afterwards that to some extent they have been wasting their time as revisions have occurred. A planned 'evolution', in which the timetable for changes will be known in advance, runs the risk that teachers will come to feel in advance that they are wasting their time. Curriculum planning blight may be the consequence of the moratorium.

Third, the protection of time spent on the basics, which Appendix I (on page 100) shows to be greater in practice than the policy guidance assumed for the national curriculum, ought not to be the main objective of the review. On the contrary, the evidence is that the national curriculum guidance embodied a more liberal and broadly–based conception of the primary curriculum than that operating in practice in the schools. Thus the prime objective of the review to 'slim down' the curriculum should be to protect time for the non–basics by showing how the basics can be planned, taught and assessed in cross–curricular applications. It thus becomes a political and ideological operation, rather than a merely mechanical exercise in excising material from statutory orders. But contrary to the received criticism that the national curriculum is narrowing down curriculum practice, the political and ideological thrust must be to persuade teachers to broaden it.

Finally, the revision process poses headteachers with some substantial dilemmas. The intention to revise, taken with the OFSTED (1993b) report and NCC (1993b) advice, might reasonably be read as an official acknowledgement that a whole curriculum of quality cannot be delivered within the given structures. Yet heads and governing bodies might equally reasonably point out that they are statutorily charged to deliver this undeliverable curriculum and, moreover, will be inspected upon the basis that it is deliverable. The next five years therefore look like being very uncomfortable ones for headteachers and governors in primary schools, unless the central policy–makers acknowledge these limits to reform, some of them arising from government policy itself.

CHAPTER THREE

KNOWLEDGE FOR TEACHING AND TEACHING PERFORMANCE

Neville Bennett, Mike Summers and Mike Askew

INTRODUCTION

The implementation of the National Curriculum has engendered a wide–ranging debate about primary school practices and their effectiveness. Prominent in initiating this debate was the discussion paper by Alexander, Rose & Woodhead (1992) which covered a wide–ranging set of issues surrounding the quality of primary teaching. Included in this set was teachers' subject knowledge. They argued that the introduction of the National Curriculum would necessitate, particularly at Key Stage 2, a substantial amount of separate subject teaching if each programme of study was to be covered. They further argued that 'good subject teaching depends upon the teachers' knowledge, skills and understanding of the subject concerned', and that this knowledge is a critical factor at every point in the teaching process: in planning, assessing, explaining and providing feedback. Although this issue had been brought into focus as a consequence of the National Curriculum they contended that HMI had been reporting a close relationship between subject knowledge and teaching quality since the 1970s.

The paper concluded that:

> 'Teachers must possess the subject knowledge which the Statutory Orders require. Without such knowledge, planning will be restricted in scope, the teaching techniques and organisational strategies employed by the teacher will lack purpose, and there will be little progression in pupils' learning.'

A logical consequence, they averred, is that the generalist primary teacher is unlikely to be able to teach all the subjects to the required level, particularly at Key Stage 2.

Publications which have followed this report have incorporated the same message. The OFSTED report (1993b), for example, stated that the headteachers and advisers who had participated in conferences to discuss the Alexander *et al.* document acknowledged that the improvement of teachers' subject knowledge was of central importance if primary schools were to make appropriate progress in teaching the National Curriculum. Similarly, NCC (1993b), in presenting advice on improving delivery of the National Curriculum, argued that one way was to provide further guidance and/or training in subjects which are currently problematic. They further argued that initial teacher training must ensure mastery of subject knowledge, but cast doubts on the efficacy of current training in this regard. This view, was, no doubt, influenced by recent HMI reports on teacher training (e.g.: 1987a, 1991) and surveys of primary teachers in the first year of teaching (1988), in which it was claimed that students, and beginning teachers, did not acquire a sufficiently broad grasp of the curriculum, or a deeper knowledge of some specialised aspects of it.

The foregoing assertions and professional judgements beg several questions, notably:

i)   what independent evidence exists to indicate that primary teachers do indeed lack subject knowledge?

ii)   does the claimed relationship between teachers' knowledge bases and teaching performances really exist?

iii)   can teachers readily acquire the knowledge they may at present lack?

The first purpose of this chapter is to review the available evidence in relation to these questions. It then moves on to consider issues and consequences arising from this review, and to suggest possible ways forward. A concluding section summarises implications for the development of future policy for the primary school curriculum, and the training of teachers.

TEACHERS' SUBJECT KNOWLEDGE

Three differing sources of evidence are available in Britain: studies of experienced teachers' understanding of science concepts; assessments of student teachers' knowledge of core curriculum subjects; and questionnaire surveys of experienced teachers' self–perceptions of subject competence.

In 1985 the DES contended that 'the greatest obstacle to the continued improvement of science in primary schools is that many existing teachers lack a working knowledge of elementary science', and this has been supported in a wide ranging set of studies on primary teachers' understanding of science concepts carried out by the Oxford based Primary School Teachers and Science Project (1988–1993). For example, Kruger and Summers (1989) reported that the majority of teachers' views were based on a 'mixture of intuitive beliefs and half–remembered textbook science from their school days, sometimes with incorrect or imprecise use of scientific language'. Another, smaller, group of teachers seemed not to possess any theoretical understanding of phenomena presented. This group had received little education in science at school and of necessity were able to explain the instances only at a perceptual level, or not at all. They concluded that the scientific thinking of many of the teachers studied resembled that of children, being limited to perceptual and observable entities.

It should be stressed that lack of knowledge is not restricted to the more traditionally difficult areas of science. For example, in a recent series of studies, widespread lack of knowledge of phenomena such as day and night, the seasons and the behaviour of the Moon has been revealed (Mant & Summers 1993, Summers & Mant forthcoming).

In their review of content knowledge for primary science teaching, Smith and Neale (1989) report that primary grade teachers are well aware of their weak backgrounds in the sciences, and that they may even hold some of the same misconceptions as their students. They suggest that it may be useful to consider teachers as adult novices in some, if not all, of the science areas they teach.

The subject knowledge of graduates entering primary PGCE courses was assessed by Bennett & Carré (1993). They devised assessments of the knowledge required for teaching based on the first six levels of the National Curriculum in Science, Maths and English.

The students' substantive and syntactic knowledge of science was limited, indicating that many did not have a bank of concepts from which they could confidently apply their knowledge to make sense of everyday phenomena. In fact many of the misconceptions described of children were apparent in these students.

The pattern in Mathematics was similar. The evidence suggests that the students did not have easy access to substantive knowledge of mathematics. They appeared to have surface knowledge, lacking in conceptual depth and an awareness of interconnections. Neither did they have a clear understanding of the syntactical nature of the subject—the process of mathematical thinking. It was thus difficult to envisage these students teaching for flexible understanding as opposed to teaching routine procedures.

The overall scores on the language items did not suggest extensive knowledge of this area. Many were unfamiliar with traditional grammar. For example, although the majority could identify verbs and nouns in sentences only a small minority could identify adverbs and pronouns. Also, although their linguistic ability appeared to be good they had difficulty with meta–linguistic aspects—i.e. to explain linguistic decisions. Finally there tended to be a lack of a technical language to discuss literature.

Improvements in knowledge for teaching did occur through the PGCE courses but they were often very small, particularly in Science and Mathematics. On the other hand students' knowledge about language improved but not their understanding of the structure of language, especially grammar.

Similar findings are reported in the United States. Ball (1990) and McDiarmid (1990) found that in the areas of Mathematics and Writing the majority of teachers and student teachers, including those who had majored in the subjects they would be teaching, had only a limited understanding of the two subjects. Moreover, in following teacher candidates through induction and in–service programmes, it was found that despite the diversity of approaches to teacher education that were studied, many of those programmes were unable to alter substantially the ideas teachers held when they arrived. Many teachers perceived school subjects not as bodies of knowledge that might be uncertain or worthy of debate, nor as relating to everyday life. Instead they perceived the two subjects, i.e. Writing and Mathematics, as 'collections of fixed rules and procedures with few connections among them and even fewer connections to events or purposes outside the classroom' (Kennedy, 1991).

A third source of data on teachers' subject knowledge has been from national questionnaire surveys of teachers' self–perceived competence to teach the National Curriculum with their present level of knowledge. Two recent surveys (Wragg, Bennett & Carré, 1989; Bennett, Wragg, Carré & Carter, 1992) show that a majority of teachers feel competent, without further help or training, in only two subjects—English and Mathematics. In the intervening period between the surveys there had been a slightly increased feeling of competence in science (from 34% to 41% of the teachers surveyed), but in most other subjects their felt competence had fallen. That in music and technology was the lowest in both surveys at 23% and 14% respectively. Similar findings, particularly in relation to science, have been reported by HMI (1989) in their consideration of the implementation of the National Curriculum—'Many teachers spoke of their own uncertain knowledge of science and their need for sustained support in this respect'.

In many of the reports referred to above their authors have inferred, like Alexander *et al.*, possible implications for teaching practice. But what evidence is there concerning the links between teachers' subject knowledge and teaching performance?

SUBJECT KNOWLEDGE AND TEACHING PERFORMANCE

Shulman (1986, 1987) was one of the first to question the ignoring of subject matter in research on classroom teaching. Missing, he argued, were questions about the content taught, the nature of the questions asked and of the explanations offered. He delineated seven knowledge bases that identify the teacher understanding needed to promote comprehension among pupils. These are:

> content Knowledge: referring to the amount and organisation of knowledge in the mind of the teacher. This includes both substantive and syntactic structure of a subject, i.e. the variety of ways in which the basic concepts and principles of the discipline are organised, and the ways in which truth or falsehood, validity or invalidity, are established.

general pedagogical knowledge: with special reference to those broad principles and strategies of classroom management and organisation that appear to transcend subject matter.

curriculum knowledge: with particular grasp of the materials and programmes that serve as 'tools of the trade' for teachers.

pedagogical content knowledge: that form of content knowledge that embodies the aspect of content most germane to its teachability. It includes, for any given subject area, the most useful forms of representation of those ideas, the most powerful analogies, illustrations, examples, explanation and demonstrations. In other words, the ways of representing and formulating the subject that make it comprehensible to others.

knowledge of learners and their characteristics.

knowledge of educational contexts: ranging from the workings of the group or classroom, the governance and financing of schools, to the character of communities and cultures.

knowledge of educational ends, purposes and values, and the philosophical and historical grounds.

Shulman views teaching through a model of pedagogical reasoning and action, represented in Figure 1.

Figure 1   *A model of pedagogical reasoning*

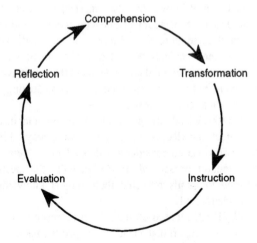

Briefly, the argument underpinning the model is that the teacher must first comprehend the ideas to be taught and the purposes to be achieved. These must then be transformed into forms which are pedagogically powerful, yet adaptive to pupil understandings. Such transformations require a combination of:-

(a)   preparation—critical scrutiny and choice of materials of instruction;
(b)   representation—a consideration of the key ideas and how they might best be represented, in the form of analogies, examples and the like;
(c)   instructional selections—choice of teaching approach; and
(d)   adaption—often called differentiation, i.e. the tailoring of input, whatever its form, to pupils' capabilities and characteristics.

Instruction, i.e. the teaching act, then takes place within a system of classroom management and organisation. The process of evaluation includes 'in–flight' checks for pupil understandings as well as more formal assessment and feedback—a process which, Shulman argues, requires all the forms of teacher comprehension and transformation described above. Reflection requires a reconstruction, re-enactment or recapturing of events and accomplishments, and is the analytic process through which a professional learns from experience. This leads back to comprehension—a new beginning.

Evidence concerning these processes and their interrelationships is emerging from recent research. Grossman *et al.* (1989) for example, report from case studies of secondary student–teachers that content knowledge affects both what teachers teach and how they teach it. Depth of knowledge also appears to influence pedagogical choices. Student–teachers with specialist knowledge were more likely to stress conceptual understanding and syntactic knowledge, whereas non-specialists simply taught the content as it was represented in the text without discussion. Organisation of knowledge also emerged as influential. Those who understood the larger map of their subject, and who understood the relationship of individual topics or skills to more general topics in their field, may also be more effective in teaching their subjects. Knowledge of syntactic structure was also important. Student–teachers who did not understand the role played by inquiry in their disciplines were not capable of adequately representing, and therefore teaching, that subject matter to their pupils.

Leinhardt *et al.* (1991) analysed good and poor mathematics teaching and concluded that subject knowledge impacted in several ways. Firstly, teacher's mental plans for lessons varied considerably dependent on their familiarity with the content to be taught (cf. Borko *et al.*, 1988). Secondly, the questions asked, and explanations offered to pupils reflected their subject knowledge, as did the representations teachers used.

McDiarmid *et al.* (1989) focused on the role of representation in pedagogical content knowledge. They report that a teacher's capacity to pose questions, select tasks, evaluate their pupils' understandings and make curriculum choices all depend on their understanding of subject matter. Teachers are better able to help pupils develop flexible understandings of subject matter if they understand the subject well. Moreover, their understandings enable teachers to develop a variety of ways of representing them to children of varying experiences and knowledge. The description of pedagogical content knowledge appropriate for primary sciences put forward by Smith and Neale (1989) includes knowledge of pupils' prior concepts, strategies for teaching content, and shaping and elaborating content (use of examples, good explanations, analogies, and so on). The importance of identifying and starting from children's existing ideas (often misconceptions) has become a plank of science education in recent years, and there is now an extensive research literature describing these preconceptions which can inform teaching (e.g.: Pfundt and Duit, 1991). However, in their review of research Smith and Neale report that primary science teachers are rarely aware of pupils' preconceptions or the power of these to interfere with science learning, and that even when informed of these ideas of pupils it is mistakenly assumed that such existing knowledge can be ignored or easily changed. This was confirmed in their own in–depth studies of elementary school teachers teaching science. They report that 'what is striking is the lack of attention to children's ideas, predictions or explanations.'

Smith and Neale (1989) also report evidence that teaching strategies to bring about conceptual change in pupils are rarely used in science lessons, and also that teachers with limited content knowledge may generate metaphors that are conceptually misleading for students. They found that 'what was missing in most of these lessons was exactly the kind of examples, analogies and metaphors which is evidence of content knowledge in use to serve pedagogical purposes'. They conclude that there is a need to address both content knowledge *per se* and pedagogical content knowledge in teacher training programmes.

Although arguing for the critical role of subject knowledge, Ball (1991) maintains that it shapes, and is shaped by, other kinds of knowledge and beliefs. Similarly, Grossman *et al.* (1989) report that student teachers' beliefs about teaching and learning are related to how they think about teaching, how they learn from their experiences, and how they conduct themselves in classrooms. They identified two types of beliefs about subjects, one about the nature of the content taught and the other, which they termed an orientation toward subject matter. These beliefs appeared to influence the content chosen for teaching, goals for instruction, and choices of activities and assignments. They concluded that prospective teachers' beliefs about subject matter are as powerful and influential as their beliefs about teaching and learning.

In the case of science, Smith and Neale (1989) identified four beliefs about the nature of science teaching, i.e. that science is a process of discovery; that science is essentially about processes and methods; that it is a body of fact and laws; or that it is about the construction and evolution of theories. They report that teachers' beliefs about the nature of science teaching is a critical component in the changes they are able to make in their teaching.

This view is supported in the latest American study to report relationships between teachers' knowledge bases and teaching performance. Putman *et al.* (1992) present case studies of fifth grade mathematics teaching and conclude that what a teacher believes about mathematics is related to how he/she views teaching and learning. If mathematics is viewed as a set of given procedures to be mastered, teaching by telling is an efficient way to convey these procedures to students. A view of mathematics as conceptual tools for understanding situations and solving problems is more consistent with a perspective of learners as constructing knowledge. These sorts of interrelated knowledge and beliefs serve as intellectual resources which teachers bring to teaching. Their concern is that most teachers hold a narrow view of mathematics i.e. that computational algorithms constitute the core of mathematics, which hinders effects to reform.

They also showed, through detailed case studies, the vital role of subject–matter knowledge in teaching for understanding, although in the examples quoted the role of knowledge was apparent through its absence.

Recent research in Britain on the relationship between knowledge for teaching and teaching performance in student teachers has reported very similar findings (Bennett & Turner–Bisset, 1993). It was hypothesized that subject knowledge for teaching would show itself in students' teaching performances. Within the sample studied this was shown to be the case. The group with high levels of appropriate subject knowledge taught that subject at consistently higher levels of competence than other students, both in the planning and interactive aspects of teaching. Case studies illustrated vividly the ways in which subject knowledge for teaching was related to all aspects of pedagogical reasoning, from the framing of intentions, through task design and representation, to evaluation and reflection. They also characterized the implications for teaching of lack of, or partial knowledge, for example, in the inability to develop or extend a theme.

The study also showed clearly that knowledge for teaching is a necessary, but not sufficient, ingredient for competent teaching performances. As in the American studies, the role of beliefs about the subject, and the role of context, were critical. Thus knowledge for teaching is clearly necessary for high quality teaching, but only if allied with other appropriate knowledge bases.

ACQUISITION OF SUBJECT AND TEACHING KNOWLEDGE

The preceding sections have summarised a body of research evidence which supports the view that primary teachers often lack knowledge and understanding of core curriculum subjects and that this adversely affects teaching performance.

The question that these findings gives rise to is the extent to which teachers can acquire the knowledge, both content and pedagogical, that they currently lack. To what extent, for example, can appropriate inservice teacher education develop the specialist subject knowledge required by the National Curriculum in the average, generalist primary school teacher? In the case of science, recent research has addressed this important question.

In England, a two–year longitudinal study of the development of 53 primary school teachers' understanding in the conceptual areas force and energy following an initial, short burst of inservice training based upon a constructivist approach has been completed recently (Summers *et al.* 1993). Courses were led in some cases by subject experts (science education lecturers in teacher training institutions), and in other cases by primary school science coordinators.

The research methodology used a variety of techniques to gain access to the teachers' conceptual understanding, including in–depth 'interviews–about–instances', questionnaires of the 'spot the expert view' type, and numerous explanation tasks. Teachers' understanding was explored prior to the inservice training, soon after the training and in the longer term (a year or so later). Principal research findings were that:

i) at the outset of the research nearly all the teachers had little scientific knowledge and understanding of the concepts of force and energy.

ii) following training all teachers had moved substantially towards the scientific view. In many cases this movement was quite remarkable, but in others the change was relatively modest.

iii) some concepts were more easily acquired than others.

iv) there was evidence of 'slipping back' i.e. marked short term gains which were no longer so evident in the longer term.

v) teachers may retain misconceptions even when these are addressed intensively during inservice training.

vi) there was evidence of a gap between teachers' perceptions of the change in their understanding and an objective assessment of this change.

viii) teachers may develop new misconceptions as a result of such training.

ix) there is a need to find ways of supporting teachers following training so that their knowledge and understanding can be reinforced and validated.

The full report of this project describes in detail concepts that were more easily understood than others, and ranks 30 such concepts, all concerned with aspects of force or energy, in order of difficulty. A key feature of the results was that inservice training, if well designed and based upon a current consensus of what constitutes good practice, can substantially improve primary teachers' understanding of science concepts. However, although greatly improved, the evidence supports the view that in many cases the scientific understanding achieved is likely to be partial and 'messy' with, for example, misconceptions coexisting alongside scientific views and teachers unsure of their new knowledge. Some teachers will progress at a greater rate than others, and some concepts will be more easily acquired than others.

This research programme was concerned mainly with developing and monitoring the development of content knowledge rather than pedagogical content knowledge, and did not involve any direct classroom observation. However, a number of teachers in the sample reported that they had now incorporated aspects of the constructivist approach they had experienced during the inservice training into their own classroom teaching of children. In particular, teachers reported that they were now eliciting children's existing views about scientific ideas and building upon these.

In the USA, Neale *et al.* (1990) report research with elementary school teachers designed to develop the content and pedagogical content knowledge necessary for implementation of conceptual change teaching. A study was made of the extent to which 8 teachers were able to implement a two week conceptual change science unit on light and shadows following a four week preparatory course. The research showed that, although there was variation in implementation among the teachers, all were able to use conceptual change teaching strategies successfully. However, Neale *et al.* do stress that these teachers had exceptionally strong support, including demonstration teaching and coaching. Also, the focus was on a single topic—a feature which they recognise as a significant strength and limitation of their training programme.

When interviewed one year later all 8 of the teachers were continuing to use the strategies they had learned, although there was some slippage. As with the English study described above, Neale *et al.* found evidence of a new emphasis on the role of pupils' conceptions, with almost all teachers in their sample reporting new sensitivity and new willingness to listen to children's ideas.

These two extensive research studies have shown how difficult it can be for primary teachers to improve their subject and teaching knowledge significantly. The evidence is that this can be done, but that extensive training and support are necessary. Even then, varying degrees of success, depending on the concepts in question, are to be expected.

An important finding for science education is the way that many primary school teachers seem to readily accept the use of pupils' ideas as starting points for teaching. But to exploit this fully teachers need to be able to anticipate the kinds of misconceptions they are likely to encounter with primary age children, and be knowledgeable about the strategies that can be used to move children towards the scientific view. These areas are ripe for research and development.

IMPLICATIONS

The evidence concerning teachers' subject knowledge suggests two areas with implications for policy and practice: teacher development and training, and curriculum implementation.

The research discussed above suggests a fundamental dilemma arising out of balancing the development of teachers' pedagogic knowledge against their subject knowledge. Current theories of the 'situated' nature of knowledge (Brown, Collins & Duguid, 1989) suggest that training environments need to be as similar as possible to the environment in which the knowledge and skills are to be used. This, in part, provides a rationale for more training time to be classroom based. A further rationale for school based training arises out of models of teaching as craft, an important requirement of student teachers being to gain access to experienced teachers' craft knowledge (Brown & McIntyre, 1992).

While such shifts in the context and focus of initial training may lead to improvements in some aspects of teaching, others could be seriously neglected. If the current state of teachers' subject knowledge is as limited as the research implies then this is likely to have an effect on school based training. The focus in schools is more likely to be on providing tips for teaching based on limited understanding of subject content, and is unlikely to develop for student teachers a rich pedagogic content knowledge.

The solution may be for higher education institutions to concentrate on subject knowledge, but this raises questions about the ability of trainees to transfer such knowledge from one context to another and suggests that developing pedagogic content knowledge can be done largely in isolation. Further, if subject knowledge were to be incorporated into one year postgraduate courses which aspects of curriculum and pedagogy would be dropped or postponed? The dilemma arises out of a shift of perception, as Kennedy (1991) argues, away from regarding teacher knowledge, both pedagogic and content, as a problem to be solved towards viewing it as a dilemma to be managed.

Kennedy believes that one approach to this dilemma is to regard teacher learning as a continuous process, a view supported by Her Majesty's Inspectorate. Initial training is increasingly seen as only a preparation for the early years of teaching, a foundation on which subsequent training and development can build. This notion of continuous teacher learning requires an understanding of the requirements of initial training, induction and INSET and 'a formal obligation laid on those responsible for each to deliver their part of the training process' (Alexander *et al.*, 1992).

Inservice teacher education is essential if there is to be an impact in the shorter term. But questions here arise as to the kind of training that will be fruitful and worth investing in. It seems to be the case that many courses are too ambitious in scope and there is a lack of awareness of how difficult it is for teacher learners to develop sound, robust understandings of new concepts and ideas. There are often unrealistic expectations in the minds of policy makers of what can be achieved in short bursts of inservice training. To develop non–trivial understanding, such courses should be more focused and extended. In science, for example, to develop an understanding of a concept such as force and associated pedagogical practices requires extended inservice provision focused on this theme. The same is true of sophisticated concepts such as energy or those required for understanding the behaviour of materials.

Teachers need both conceptual understanding and pedagogical knowledge and skills, and it is important that both are considered when planning inservice provision. In addition, there is evidence to suggest that teachers' beliefs about subjects and about the teaching and learning of subjects may be important influences on classroom teaching. This is an area which merits explicit attention in inservice courses, but there is little research evidence to inform practice.

Evidence also suggests that teachers need continuing help after attending a course—help which will enable them, for example, to validate their knowledge when they come to plan work for children or after they have taught material and need debriefing. In the UK this kind of ongoing support (e.g. through the use of advisory teachers servicing a number of schools) has been reduced considerably in recent years, despite evidence of its value (e.g.: ASE 1993). Ways thus need to be found of providing support of this kind.

The notion of continuous teacher learning suggests the need for a baseline from which to work and towards which to aim. Work has already begun on the development of broad–based core teaching competencies providing teachers with a competency profile achieved on exit from initial training (cf. Dunne & Harvard, 1993). Further research needs to be carried out developing such profiles to delineate which aspects might be targeted at each phase of training and to inform the design and implementation of training courses.

The issue of subject knowledge needs careful consideration within competency based models of training. Given the National Curriculum is it feasible or desirable to try to train primary teachers for all 10 subjects? If the evidence available with respect to science extends to other subjects then perhaps the generalist model of the primary school teacher does need to be examined carefully for tenability within the current curriculum. The development of individual teachers' subject competencies may need to be linked with school development planning and a clearer consideration of what INSET is needed for members of staff in relation to staff subject expertise as a whole. Differentiated courses for teachers with different levels of knowledge may be one solution but this presents difficulties over targeting and funding. Teacher educators must address the same issues and develop and implement more flexible programmes to allow, for example, self diagnosis and evaluation of subject knowledge and independent learning units addressing the knowledge required for teaching different levels and areas of the curriculum.

One further solution to the issue of teacher subject knowledge could involve reducing the curriculum to those aspects teachers can more readily understand. While this cannot be a complete solution to the problem, there are ways in which the curriculum might be made more manageable and possibly reduce demands on teachers' subject knowledge. For example, the introduction and use of measures cuts across mathematics, science and design & technology. The identification and consolidation of areas of the curriculum where there is such overlap could help reduce the perceived curriculum overload at Key Stage 2. Future reviews of the National Curriculum may need to consider whether strict delineation by subject is always necessary.

An alternative approach is to identify the concepts within the primary curriculum that teachers need to understand, i.e. the substantive content knowledge required, together with an analysis and specification of the level of understanding to be achieved. It would also be necessary to identify appropriate pedagogical content knowledge in relation to the particular ideas and concepts to be taught. At primary level, there appears to be relatively little research evidence to inform practice. Key questions thus arise of how pedagogical content knowledge is to be generated and disseminated.

Consideration must also be given to the issue of specialist v non–specialist teaching. Although on the surface the advantages of pupils being taught by teachers with sound subject knowledge may outweigh the disadvantages, the actual implementation of such a solution needs examining. Apart from the challenge posed to the prevailing culture of primary schools, difficulties in staffing such an approach operate at two levels: first, whether or not the profession can attract specialists, particularly in the sciences; second, whether the sizes of primary schools make it possible to staff them in ways which enable the curriculum to be adequately covered. An alternative is to enable teachers with subject specialisms to work alongside colleagues. This has the potential for non–specialist teachers to have their pedagogic content knowledge extended, and be enacted within a school based INSET programme.

Nevertheless, any moves towards more subject based teaching are likely to be long term, and in the short term teachers' insecure knowledge, particularly in mathematics and science, makes likely their continued reliance upon commercial materials to implement the curriculum. There is thus a burden on publishers to produce materials which are educationally valid, utilising the most appropriate representations.

It is not easy to be optimistic in the prevailing climate about the future support teacher and schools will receive for developing the knowledge bases necessary for

high quality teaching of the National Curriculum. A number of suggestions for
ways forward have been made above, but recent developments may militate
against these. So, for example, it seems inevitable that the length of BEd teacher
training courses will diminish from four to three years, putting even greater strain
on students' acquisition of the necessary knowledge bases for teaching, a strain
already present in the overloaded PGCE programmes. Neither is it possible to
foresee improvements in the quality of induction, or inservice courses. Indeed
many schools appear unable to fund any but the shortest inservice courses
available, which, by their very length and nature, are unlikely to significantly
affect practice. Thus the notion of continued teacher development, although
accepted by all in theory, is likely to be emaciated in practice.

CHAPTER FOUR

WHOLE SCHOOL PLANNING IN THE PRIMARY SCHOOL

Hilary Burgess, Geoff Southworth and Rosemary Webb

INTRODUCTION

In recent years the concept of 'whole school' has been increasingly used to signal the belief that teachers should plan and work together. With the introduction of the 1988 Education Act, whole school planning has become an important element of teachers' work in primary schools. For example, the National Curriculum Council advocated in its Curriculum Guidance One document, "A Framework for the Primary Curriculum" (NCC, 1989a) that curriculum planning needs to be at three levels, whole school, class and individual pupil. However, the increasingly popular rhetoric of 'whole school' has not been matched by detailed practical guidance as to what it means or looks like in practice.

In this paper we will explore some of the issues surrounding whole school planning, especially at Key Stage 2. In the first section we will focus on the notion of whole school. In the second section we will look at curriculum planning. In the third section we will consider the implications of whole school planning for teachers' and headteachers' roles and responsibilities. Lastly, we will outline our conclusions and set out some recommendations.

'WHOLE SCHOOLS'

Nias, Southworth and Yeomans (1989) have shown that staff in primary schools relate positively to one another where there exists within the school an organizational culture of collaboration. A culture of collaboration rests upon:

> 'four interacting beliefs. The first two specify ends: individuals should be valued but, because they are inseparable from the groups of which they are a part, groups too should be fostered and valued. The second two relate to means: the most effective ways of promoting these values are through openness and a sense of mutual security.' (Nias *et al.*, 1989, p. 47)

The existence of these beliefs and the resulting school culture make it possible for heads, teachers and other staff routinely and unselfconsciously to work as a team and despite their differences to strive to achieve common goals. The culture, since it reflects and embodies the dual values of individuals and groups, facilitates the coexistence of both teacher independence and staff interdependence.

School effectiveness studies have shown that teacher collaboration benefits the pupils and the school. For example, Mortimore *et al.*'s (1988) study concludes that the involvement of the deputy head in school management activities and the involvement of teachers in curriculum planning are two factors which contribute to the overall effectiveness of the school. More recently, Bolam *et al.*'s (1993) enquiry into teachers' views about school effectiveness demonstrates that heads and teachers recognise the value of teamwork, professional openness and collegiality.

School improvement studies generally reach the same conclusions. Fullan (1991) claims that collegiality among teachers (measured by the frequency of communication, mutual support, help etc.) was a strong indicator of the implementation success of planned changes. Consequently, Fullan and Hargreaves (1992) argue that what is worth fighting for in schools is a sense of what they call 'total schools'. By total school they mean schools which have collaborative cultures and where there is much professional interaction, development and interdependence. HM Inspectors have also stressed the importance of teachers working together. They have referred to primary staff groups as 'combined teaching units' (HMI, 1987b) and through promoting the work of curriculum co-ordinators have emphasised the benefits of staff sharing their subject strengths and interests.

Much of the above is also supported by two other studies. Nias, Southworth and Campbell (1992) have investigated whole school curriculum development in primary schools. Their study shows that a collaborative culture:

> 'is a necessary condition for whole school curriculum development, because it creates trust, security and openness. Yet, these are not sufficient conditions for growth. For growth to take place, at the level of either the individual or the school, teachers must also be constantly learning.' (p. 247).

To avoid collaboration becoming too comfortable or complacent, it needs to include and facilitate members of staff learning with and from one another, as well as from colleagues outside the school.

Much the same findings can be seen in Rosenholtz's (1989) work. In her study of 78 elementary schools in Tennesee, Rosenholtz describes the workplace conditions of the schools in terms of 'stuck' and 'moving''. Stuck schools were not supportive of change and development and were characterised as places where the teachers worked in isolation, did not support one another and did not value one another. Consequently, these were schools where there was little opportunity for teachers to develop by working with their colleagues and Rosenholtz called them 'learning impoverished' settings (p. 81). By contrast, in 'moving' schools teachers worked together more and they believed that teaching was inherently difficult and that everyone needed help sometimes. This meant that teachers communicated with one another and offered help and support to each other. In turn, teacher growth and improvement was regarded as a collective enterprise and not an individualised one. According to Rosenholtz, 'moving' schools are 'learning enriched' settings (p. 80).

There is, then, much evidence to support the idea of teachers collaborating and strong arguments can be mounted for schools to become cohesive and interdependent communities of developing teachers. Yet it also needs to be acknowledged that whilst there is a strong case for whole schools, they are not easily established or sustained. The whole school curriculum development project (Nias *et al.*, 1992) showed that whole schools need to be actively created and maintained. Leaders, that is heads and other school leaders, need to model a willingness to work with colleagues and exhibit a desire to keep on learning and developing as professionals. Furthermore, the following conditions need to be nurtured since these facilitate whole school curriculum development:

shared institutional values (valuing learning, teamwork, interdependence and compromise)

organizational structures (for learning together, working together, decision–making, communication)

resources (time, commitment, people and materials) (see Nias *et al.*, 1992, pp. 198–224).

Whole school curriculum development is also fragile and full of tension. It is fragile because it relies on the above conditions to be in place and for them to continue to exist. Yet, because these are prone to change, as staff turnover occurs and the circumstances within the school alter, whole school development can be impeded or set back. It is full of tension because the more staff interact, the more likely it becomes that their professional and interpersonal differences will be noticed and, perhaps, aggravated. Collaboration is likely to increase the micropolitical dimension of the workplace. Staff will need to handle the differences which exist between themselves and be able to resolve them. They will also need to reach workable solutions to problems and this means they will all have to engage in interpersonal and inter–professional negotiations and accept some measure of compromise.

There is one other major reason why developing whole schools and engaging in whole school planning is difficult. Staff collaboration is not easily compatible with the organizational structures and customs of many primary schools (Nias *et al.*, 1989). Organizational structures have sustained occupational norms of professional autonomy, territoriality, isolation and independence. Indeed, for many teachers information about pupils and the practice of other teachers is based upon an assumed 'shared knowledge' (Burgess, 1985) rather than upon a discussion of aims, procedures and practice. Many teachers are unaccustomed to working with their colleagues. They may socially interact with them, but this should not be mistaken for collaboration, let alone a sense of 'whole school'.

While the prospects for whole school planning are not promising, the outlook is certainly not entirely pessimistic. A number of factors now encourage staff in schools to work together more than in previous years. First, the school closure days for INSET have enabled staff groups to work together on topics and tasks of common concern. Second, the introduction of LMS, open enrolment, and competition for pupils—in short the 'market forces' ideology—has possibly generated stronger internal collaboration and teamwork. Third, the introduction of teacher appraisal has enabled staff to visit colleagues' classrooms and has encouraged peer observation. Fourth, mentoring for newly qualified teachers has also encouraged stronger ties between teachers. Fifth, school development planning in some schools has encouraged greater staff consultation and shared decision-making. Sixth, the introduction of the National Curriculum has forced primary teachers to rely on colleagues and to co–ordinate with them to an unusual extent. As Hargreaves (1992) says, the weaknesses of a culture of individualism are exposed by the advent of the National Curriculum since its successful implementation requires from teachers new attitudes and practices and ones which are incompatible with a culture which prizes individualism:

> 'To survive in the National Curriculum world, the primary teacher is under pressure to learn not merely to coexist with and be friendly to colleagues, but to collaborate with them.' (Hargreaves 1992, p. 5)

Whole school curriculum planning and development then may be happening almost by accident rather than design. To ensure that the benefits of whole school approaches are more systematically encouraged, staff in primary schools will need to be better equipped to manage the processes on which whole school planning and development rely and this means that there needs to be INSET available to support those who wish to work in collaborative settings.

CURRICULUM PLANNING

The idea of whole school curriculum planning has opened up a new field where the terms are still being defined despite the early assimilation of phrases such as 'whole school', 'whole curriculum' and 'development planning' into the language of primary schooling. However, planning for teaching in primary schools is not new and the past two decades have witnessed a number of phases in the development of curriculum planning.

During the late 1970s and early 1980s teachers were encouraged to develop written statements of curriculum aims (DES 1981, Thomas 1985), and many local education authorities began to produce curriculum guidelines for schools. Teachers were introduced to programmes of school–based self–evaluation and review (Simons 1987, Clift *et al.* 1987) where the emphasis was upon individual school planning while research on school effectiveness and improvement (Rutter *et al.* 1979 and Mortimore *et al.* 1988) has promoted a systematic approach to planning and review and provided evidence to support the need for school development planning (Hargreaves and Hopkins 1991).

From the late 1970s onwards HMI have identified weaknesses in planning at both school and classroom level. Alexander *et al.* (1992) point out that 'much school planning in areas other than mathematics and reading (where published schemes provided a not always appropriate prop) amounted to little more than an attempt to list the content to be covered' (p. 20) which resulted in insufficient attention being given to continuity and progression. The introduction of the National Curriculum was viewed as 'having a positive influence on curricular planning', fostering both 'long term strategic planning and shorter term preparations related particularly to work in the core subjects' (HMI 1989, p. 3). However, the extent and detail of National Curriculum planning met resistance from teachers who felt that they were 'document driven' and 'treading the narrow path' and had lost the spontaneity and flexibility to respond to children's interests and unanticipated learning opportunities (Osborn and Pollard 1991, Pollard *et al.* 1994, Webb 1993a). Initially topic work—often including aspects of several subjects—was the focus of much whole school planning for the National Curriculum. Existing topics were mapped against the attainment targets (ATs) and to a lesser extent the programmes of study (PoS) and these were modified and new topics created to provide subject coverage and progression through the ATs and statements of attainment (SoAs) via successive topics. However, in order to be confident that National Curriculum requirements were met and to assess and record individual achievement of the SoAs, increasingly, especially at Key Stage 2, topic work has become more subject focused and more subjects and aspects of subjects are taught separately (for an analysis of the changing nature of topic work see Dadds 1993, Webb 1993). As acknowledged by OFSTED (1993b) 'the sum of the subject parts constituted an unmanageable whole for the typical primary teacher' (p.15). Whichever approaches to curriculum organisation were adopted Webb's (1993a) research into the implementation of the National Curriculum at Key Stage 2 showed that, the content proved impossible to fit into the teaching time available and depth and quality were being sacrificed in the pursuit of breadth. However, attempts at least to achieve coverage, at the level of documentation, led to extremely complex plans especially in schools with mixed–age and mixed–key stage classes where plans are on two and four year cycles. The demands of such planning combined with those of assessment and record keeping created stressful and unattainable workloads for teachers which detracted from the professional gains of such corporate efforts.

Whilst primary teachers have long been accustomed to planning they have been less used to planning at the whole school level, and, of course, are relatively unaccustomed to working within the National Curriculum framework. Teachers can thus be viewed as doubly disadvantaged. They need to learn how to plan an unwieldy and unmanageable curriculum, especially at Key Stage 2, and many must simultaneously learn to plan with their colleagues. The content and processes of whole school planning are new to many teachers.

Staff in schools have generally responded to these new demands by holding many more meetings in and after school. However, there are two difficulties with this strategy. First, Campbell and Neill's (1992) research shows that many teachers have resented the increase in staff meetings because it has been seen as at the expense of their much needed lesson preparation time. Second, the extent that staffroom discussion and policy–making affects classroom practice depends upon more than consultative decision making (Nias *et al.* 1992; Fullan 1991). Head teachers and curriculum leaders need to play an active role in monitoring the implementation of collective decisions in individual classrooms. Teachers who are not wholly committed to decisions and policies agreed by staff may ignore them in practice.

The style of management of the headteacher may also have a major influence upon the way in which staff interpret school policy. Traditionally headteachers have had the final say on matters of school policy (Coulson 1980; Campbell 1985) and their right of veto may inhibit the extent to which staff participate in decision making and adversely affect their commitment to school policy. For example, the London Institute School Development Plan project suggests that some school development plans are headteacher development plans. Therefore, it is important that we now consider the roles and responsibilities of heads and teachers in the post 1988 period.

CHANGING ROLES AND RESPONSIBILITIES

A range of research and advice exists which examines the role of the headteacher prior to the Education Reform Act (ERA) (1988)—for example, Clerkin, 1985; Craig *et al.* 1990; Kent, 1989, Paisey and Paisey 1987; Price & Reid, 1989. However, the ERA has forced multiple innovations to be rapidly implemented (Wallace, 1992), placing many additional demands on headteachers, especially in small schools where there are very few teachers with whom to share the workload.

Headteachers' availability to be involved in curriculum development and teaching has been curtailed particularly by the increased burden of administration associated with LMS. This has been further exacerbated in cases where headteachers have had to familiarise themselves with computer systems and software packages installed to facilitate the new management systems. Headteachers are also coming to terms with additional governor powers, providing school–based INSET, teacher appraisal and competing in the market place for pupils as a result of open enrolment. Associated with each of these elements has been an increase in documentation to read, forms to be filled in, meetings to be attended, decisions to be made and policies to be drawn up. While all these areas of headteachers' work are interrelated, and therefore complementary, they can be viewed as in conflict because they exert competing demands on time.

Webb (forthcoming) in her research into the implementation of the National Curriculum at Key Stage 2 in fifty schools found that all the headteachers held visions of what they would like their schools to become, maintained an overview of the curriculum and informally evaluated initiatives. However, there was enormous variation in the extent to which headteachers made a direct contribution to one or more aspects of the review, planning, teaching and monitoring of the National Curriculum subjects. For headteachers of small schools and those with almost full–time class commitments the curriculum was a central concern because it affected their teaching and their daily interactions with pupils. As they familiarised themselves with the Orders, they tried to translate the requirements into realistic classroom practice. In small schools the documentation for schemes of work and subject policy statements gradually evolved as, and when, there was time to work on them or were developed jointly with other schools in their cluster. In medium and large schools most headteachers assumed some curricular responsibilities, although they often found their intentions hard to realise in practice. Many headteachers considered that they did not have the same knowledge of the Orders as their staff nor the same confidence and experience in teaching the newer aspects of some subjects. This both reduced their credibility and their ability to provide curriculum leadership in terms of making recommendations and leading by example. It also made it difficult to continue with the lessons planned by class teachers when they covered for absent staff at short notice. Those, who had not had a regular teaching commitment for two to three years owing to the demands of the ERA, felt deskilled and were concerned that they were no longer effective and exemplary teachers. Consequently, much of the 'practical nuts and bolts' work of curriculum leadership was delegated to deputy headteachers, key stage co-ordinators and/or curriculum co–ordinators. Headteachers in the largest schools had delegated the majority or all of their curriculum responsibilities.

In larger schools in the sample 'senior management teams' including the deputy head and the allowance holders had been formed to speed up and streamline the decision–making process. The strengthening or creation of hierarchies in order to cope with the pace and amount of externally imposed change can be viewed as in conflict with staff participation and ownership of curriculum policies. Increasingly, all headteachers were aware of their role as team builders and the need to develop appropriate interpersonal and managerial skills. In some schools the National Curriculum was viewed as bringing about a new openness to share concerns and ideas and to make decisions cooperatively while in others it was viewed as legitimating and strengthening the collegial management approach that was already in place. However, several heads confided that, while sharing at the level of whole school planning had been relatively easy to achieve, getting teachers to work together and 'open their classroom doors' was proving much more difficult. In contrast to most schools which aspired to introduce changes through staff working cooperatively several headteachers spoke of how they had used the National Curriculum as a manipulative device to 'get teachers who had got somewhat set in their ways to start to move' and to bring about curriculum changes that they felt were long overdue. However, the effect of continual changes to the Orders was resulting in teachers, who were unwilling to change 'digging in their heels' and feeling justified in waiting 'until things settle down'. Those teachers, who had taken the lead in making changes, were viewed by headteachers as in danger of becoming disillusioned or suffering from innovation fatigue. All headteachers stressed the increased need, as a result of the pressures and anxieties of the implementation of the National Curriculum and its assessment arrangements, to spend time counselling staff.

While there is a wealth of literature on headship there appears to be relatively little on the role of the deputy headteacher. Mortimer *et al.* (1988) provide a picture of the role of deputy heads prior to the ERA. They found that for most deputies—three–quarters of whom were also class teachers—'the most important part of their role was connected in some way with the interpersonal relationships between the headteachers, teachers, parents and pupils' (p. 51). The other main aim cited by one fifth of deputies concerned 'the creation of good standards' and several also emphasised the need to be able 'to take over and fill in for anybody' (p. 51). Interestingly, as in the study by Mortimer *et al.* the 'socio–emotional role' as 'an encourager or counsellor to the staff' was viewed as the major part of the deputy heads' role in over two–thirds of the 31 questionnaire returns from deputies received by Purvis and Dennison (1993, p. 17). However, Purvis and Dennison found that deputies made a major contribution to the school curriculum as 'all bar three reported that their job descriptions involved co–ordination of a National Curriculum area—12 for more than one area; with twice as many claiming a major involvement with whole school curriculum development in a management role' (p.17).

In Webb's (forthcoming) research all deputies fulfilled some of what they described as the deputy's 'traditional nuts and bolts jobs' such as running sports days, putting out the chairs for assembly and arranging school visits. However, nearly all the deputies were co–ordinators of one or more subjects—usually including a core subject. Several were also the school's INSET co–ordinator. In the larger schools some had oversight of all the Key Stage 2 curriculum or had been delegated the practical work and managerial responsibility of curriculum leadership for the school. The majority of the deputy headteachers in the sample were also full–time class teachers who were given between one lesson and one day a week of non–contact time to carry out their extra duties. A few 'floating' deputies were able to provide non–contact time for class teachers, specialist subject lessons and support for pupils with special educational needs. However, the increasing concern to keep class size down to reduce teachers' workloads and improve school marketability meant that there were very few 'floating' deputies.

The contribution that teachers with particular subject expertise might make to curriculum leadership in the primary school has been increasingly acknowledged since the growing demands on class teachers made by the expanding primary curriculum caused The Plowden Report (CACE, 1967) to propose that 'teachers expert in the main field of learning should give advice to their colleagues throughout the school' (para. 556). Reynolds and Saunders (1987) carried out research into the responses of primary schools in one LEA to their LEA policy documentation and subject guidelines. They concluded that co–ordinator impact on school practice was enhanced by the following:

> frequent informal discussion of planning with colleagues;
> demonstration of teaching strategies ('change by example'), often in
> the co–ordinators own classroom;
> offering curriculum content and materials;
> 'high profile' head teacher support, especially in juggling time
> allocations or providing resources, and in expressing public approval;

and, not least,

> 'grafting' and generally, 'putting oneself about' in a non–interfering
> way. (p. 207)

However, like Campbell (1985) in his study of school–based curriculum development in eight primary schools, they found that 'it was striking that curriculum discussion, policy formulation, and action had to be "fitted into" routine classroom and school commitments, resulting in long periods of inaction, with short bursts of activity.' (p. 205).

The workload involved in planning the National Curriculum has resulted in most teachers becoming curriculum co–ordinators for one or more National Curriculum subjects. Many also have additional co–ordinating responsibilities for areas such as Key Stage 1, Key Stage 2, assessment, special educational needs, home/school liaison and in–service. Only some teachers receive incentive allowances for this work and temporary allowances—sometimes awarded on a competitive basis—can vary in duration from one term to two years. In small schools, where teachers are each co–ordinating several subjects, it is impossible for them to develop adequate knowledge and expertise in order to lead effectively.

Webb (forthcoming) found that most subject co–ordinators went on appropriate courses and fed information back to staff. However, there was often insufficient time for this to happen as only those whose subjects were in the process of being reviewed and developed could have prime time on school training days. Co–ordinators led working parties or whole–school discussions to revise or develop policy documents. They reviewed plans for teaching their subject throughout the school in order to ensure that National Curriculum requirements were covered and that there was no repetition and suggested ideas and resources. The majority of co–ordinators kept a check on resources and either recommended to the head or the deputy, whoever had oversight of resources, what should be purchased or managed the budget and ordering for that subject themselves. Co–ordinators viewed resource management as a straightforward administrative task which could be done alone, was non–threatening, and was appreciated by staff for its practical value. As in the study by Reynolds and Saunders, co–ordinators sought predominantly to influence practice indirectly through 'grafting' and meeting teachers' practical needs. Interestingly, Moore (1992), who analysed questionnaire responses from 222 primary heads (a return rate of 44.4%) on the role of the science co–ordinator, found considerable imbalance between identifying the need for, and obtaining, resources and assisting colleagues in their use.

Co–ordinators seldom worked alongside colleagues and the main reason given for this was the lack of non–contact time needed for this to happen. However, co–ordinators felt that even given the opportunity, initially it might be difficult to instigate as teachers still lacked confidence in, and experience of, sharing their classroom practice with others. Some young co–ordinators were concerned about trying to influence the practice of older and more senior members of staff. Moore (1992) suggests that lack of classroom–based support in science was also derived from a belief held by many headteachers that co–ordinators should not make decisions affecting the classroom actions of colleagues. Similarly, in their study of the role of science co–ordinators in five primary schools Kinder and Harland (1991) found that science co–ordinators were not expected to have a direct influence on classroom practice. They found that headteachers regarded co–ordinators as a 'support package' which teachers could choose whether or not to draw on at their own discretion. A decade on from the research undertaken in 1980–82 by Campbell (1985) notions of teachers' autonomy and headteacher authority in curricular matters still appear a constraint on cooperative working.

CONCLUSIONS AND RECOMMENDATIONS

Whole school planning in primary schools is now a central feature of primary school teachers' work; it identifies problematic areas of curriculum planning and staff collaboration, while providing direction for school and staff development. In the final section of this chapter we will consider some of the conclusions that can be drawn from recent research and propose recommendations for improving practice in primary schools.

Research conducted before and after the ERA shows that whole school planning rests upon a collaborative school culture. Such a culture is only created when staff: aspire to belong to a community; share the same educational beliefs and aims; work as a team to implement school policies; play an individual role within the team; call upon one another's expertise; relate well to each other; acknowledge the concerns of their colleagues; value the leadership of the headteacher; and are supported and encouraged by the headteacher. A collaborative culture based upon these premises takes time to develop and whilst many schools may be socially cohesive, not all of these have shifted from cultures of independence to ones of professional interdependence. Collaboration may be more of an aspiration than an achievement. It is important to analyse the roles and interrelationships of all those staff in schools who make a key contribution to whole school planning, such as headteachers, deputy headteachers and curriculum co-ordinators, and to explore the implications of these for their wellbeing and effectiveness.

The headteacher's leadership is vital to the creation of a collaborative culture and whole school planning and policy implementation. However, the belief that all primary headteachers, irrespective of the size of school, should teach and be curriculum leaders may be ideologically sound but practically impossible. The demands of the ERA have greatly increased the administrative and managerial elements of a head's role and it seems likely that these will predominate in many medium and large schools unless there are changes in the current level of funding and in staffing structures. As Handy and Aitkin (1986) have pointed out, in other organisations 'the higher you rise in an organisation the greater the proportion of the managerial element in your life' (p. 35) and you are not expected to continue to carry out the operational elements that you once did. It may be unreasonable and unnecessary to expect headteachers to acquire the new skills they need to fulfil their current range of roles and yet still maintain those that they developed as a class teacher. Greater attention needs to be given to the structural diversity of primary provision and the identification and development of alternative models of headship and managing primary schools which take account of this diversity.

If headteachers of larger schools are to continue to be practising and effective teachers, a way forward is for them to exchange some of their administrative and executive functions for the classroom duties of their deputies and curriculum co–

ordinators. This would heighten staff awareness of other aspects of school life, give them more ownership of decision making and improve their promotion prospects. However, given that there is little slack in the system, further delegation and sharing of duties could prove dysfunctional for both the head and the teachers because efficiency and competency seem likely to decrease if time has to be spread ever more thinly and in piecemeal manner across an even wider range of tasks.

Deputy headteachers have maintained the work traditionally expected of them while taking on new responsibilities. As argued by Harrison and Gill (1992) the knowledge and expertise of many deputies appears to make them better fitted for the role of curriculum leader than the headteachers. However, the majority of them are class teachers and consequently do not have the opportunity to monitor the curriculum in action across the whole school. Also, because of the steady expansion of their duties, in many cases they appear overstretched and their class teaching is suffering. The role of the deputy head clearly needs to be thought through in each school and the deputy's job description and its relationship to the role of the head negotiated and made explicit.

Curriculum co-ordinators are playing a major role in whole school planning and raising the collective confidence of staff in their subjects. However, their opportunities to provide curriculum leadership and their impact on classroom practice are limited by lack of non-contact time to carry out their responsibilities and to work alongside their colleagues. The DES discussion paper (Alexander *et al.*, 1992) highlighted the unjustifiable discrepancy between the funding of Y6 and Y7 pupils and argued that this reduced primary schools' flexibility to make best use of their staff. Arguments defending the disparity are that historically primary schools have always been funded at a lower rate than secondary schools and that secondary schools need more generous funding to provide time for teachers to plan and to mark work and to operate specialist teaching where classes and teachers interchange. These arguments are erroneous. Expectations of primary schools' teachers have been growing over the decades and the introduction of the National Curriculum both further extends expectations and makes these explicit. Primary teachers have an increasing amount of preparation, assessment and record keeping to do and have to reorganise their classrooms and resources during each day to provide for practical work in different subjects. Their need for the time to accomplish this is no less than their secondary counterparts.

As we write in late 1993, an all-party House of Commons Select Committee is currently conducting an inquiry into the funding issue. It is vital that extra money is made available to primary schools if subject co-ordinators, who are also class teachers, are to have the opportunity to further develop their roles and deputy heads are to be able to fulfil their classroom and curriculum leadership responsibilities more effectively. Power to reduce the present disparity lies mainly with central government. The Department for Education must acknowledge its responsibilities for leadership on this issue and initiate action rather than pretend it is a matter for local government to resolve.

While lack of funding limits whole school planning and implementation, aspects of the traditional primary school culture, which sustained teacher professional autonomy, independence and isolation, continue to constrain the impact that teachers can have on the practice of their colleagues. A collaborative school culture, where teachers share beliefs and aims and have developed ways of working as a team, takes time to develop. However, the current reforms have resulted in the largely unintended consequence of bringing teachers together to share anxieties and ideas and to plan ways forward together. Cooperation at the level of policy–making and planning is increasingly valued and now ways need to be found to extend this cooperation into the classroom.

CHAPTER FIVE

TEACHING AND LEARNING PROCESSES

Pam Sammons, Ann Lewis, Maggie MacLure, Jeni Riley,
Neville Bennett and Andrew Pollard

INTRODUCTION

The focus of this paper is an analysis of the likely consequences at Key Stage 2
(Key Stage 2) of the implementation of the National Curriculum upon teaching
and learning processes in primary schools. It should be recognised, however, that
overlap and interconnections exist with other areas considered in this book,
especially knowledge for teaching and teaching performance. In addition, there
are close links with the analysis of the impact of the National Curriculum on
provision for children with special educational needs (see Chapter 6 of this
volume).

The National Curriculum at Key Stage 2 is not, as yet, fully implemented. There
is considerable controversy over the role and nature of national testing arrangements
and doubt over their implementation. Also proposals by the National Curriculum
Council (NCC 1993b) and Office for Standards in Education (OFSTED 1993b) to
revise the National Curriculum for primary schools are likely to have significant
implications for the curriculum delivery at Key Stage 2 in particular (e.g. the stress
on more specialist subject teaching, ability setting and the use of whole class
instruction). The proposal that the ten National Curriculum subjects need to be
revised on a rolling programme every five years and recognition that the teacher's
work load (in terms of statutory learning targets) has caused significant problems
at Key Stage 1 are also likely to lead to important changes in National Curriculum
requirements at Key Stage 2.

There is also doubt about the framework for national testing particularly in
relation to the number of levels and their relationship to progression and
development over time in different subjects. The teachers' boycott of national
testing this summer and the Government's acceptance of the recommendations
made by Sir Ron Dearing, the Chairman of the new School Curriculum and
Assessment Authority (SCAA) in his interim report *The National Curriculum and
its Assessment* (Dearing 1993), have major implications for the implementation of
the National Curriculum. There appears to have been a major shift in Government
policy acknowledging the need for greater consultation and cooperation with the
teaching profession. The abandoning of plans for league tables at age seven and

fourteen; the reduction in time for the compulsory curriculum and recognition of additional time for optional lessons; plans for fewer and shorter tests in the core areas of English, mathematics and science only; the upgrading of teacher assessment; and acceptance of the need for more research into 'value-added' measures of the performance of pupils and schools are changes which will be generally welcomed by practitioners.

Given the fact that the National Curriculum at Key Stage 2 is not fully implemented and that current requirements are in the process of significant change, in considering the likely consequences of its implementation it is only possible to utilise empirical evidence and conclusions derived from previous research or research in progress and to offer insights based on such analyses, historical precedents and experience elsewhere. It is not, as yet, possible to present any hard evidence concerning actual effects for this age group.

Seven topics of relevance to the likely consequences of implementing the National Curriculum for classroom context are identified. These are the organisation of pupils' and teachers' activities and time, pupil learning; language; pupil experiences; assessment, resources and entitlement. Each of these topics is examined in relation to likely consequences (both positive and negative) of the implementation of the National Curriculum at Key Stage 2 as it is currently specified and in the light of Government acceptance of the recommendations made by Sir Ron Dearing in his interim report (Dearing 1993).

CLASSROOM ORGANISATION

Classroom organisation has always been an issue of immense importance to teachers because it is a central means through which educational aims are transformed into practice. At a technical level, this involves the production of a coherent classroom strategy by which space, pupils, time, resources, tasks and activities can be coordinated and this is, in itself, a highly skilled activity. Beyond that though, the form of organisation in each classroom, and the nature of its implementation and maintenance, has considerable social implications for teacher-pupil relationships. This is manifested by both overt and taken-for-granted rules or conventions which, by framing behaviour and expectations, can have a considerable influence on the quality of both teacher and pupil experiences. In a sense, they represent a 'culture' for each classroom. Primary school teachers in England have taken a particular pride in the provision of caring and enabling classroom cultures for educational as well as social reasons.

The implementation of the National Curriculum has considerable implications for the ways teachers go about the task of organising pupils' curriculum and learning experiences, their interactions with pupils and the way they manage classroom activity and pupil behaviour. It is likely that some aspects of change will (or could in certain circumstances) have beneficial consequences for children. There is certainly evidence that many primary teachers have reacted fairly favourably to the framework, coherence and direction provided by the National Curriculum (in a way which was not predicted at its inception), although not to the excessive workload and assessment requirements. In addition to possible benefits, however, the potential for adverse consequences for both children and teachers also needs to be recognised (Pollard *et al.* 1994).

In terms of approaches to teaching it seems probable that more emphasis may be given to single subject teaching as the National Curriculum is implemented at Key Stage 2, particularly if the NCC's (1993b) proposals on the need for, and value of, increasing the use of single subject teaching and of specialist subject teachers are accepted. Indeed, evidence for this has already been found at Key Stage 1 (Pollard *et al.* 1994). There is some research evidence which indicates that teachers can have great difficulties in successfully managing children's learning in sessions where work on several different curriculum areas is ongoing. In particular, lower levels of work–related teacher–pupil communication and more routine administrative interactions, and lower levels of pupil engagement in work activity have been reported in primary school research studies (Mortimore *et al.* 1988; Alexander 1992).

If, as the available research evidence suggests, teachers who organise mixed curriculum activities in the same sessions for a large proportion of the school day spend more time on routine classroom management than teachers who organise children to work within a single curriculum area, then a move towards more subject–based teaching might help to increase the amount of active learning time for children and assist teachers to focus more on work–related than on administrative activities.

It is also possible that the subject framework provided by the National Curriculum and the use of TA and SATs may help to ensure greater equality in curriculum coverage both between schools and between different classes of the same age group in the same school. Work by Bennett *et al.* (1984) and Bennett (1992) has demonstrated wide variations in curriculum coverage for pupils within the same class and in different schools. Likewise, Tizard *et al.*'s (1988) work on infant schools revealed:

> 'a wide range between schools or classes in what children of the same age were taught, and this could not be accounted for by the intake of the school' (p 172).

Tizard *et al.* concluded that, to some extent, limited curriculum coverage was related to low teacher expectations both of which affected infant children's progress and attainment negatively. The importance of curriculum coverage was emphasised:

> 'it is clear that attainment and progress depend crucially on whether children are given particular learning experiences' (p 172).

More emphasis on whole–class teaching could also result from the implementation of the National Curriculum. There is some research evidence that the adoption of whole class instruction can lead to greater levels of overall pupil–teacher interaction with all children. Gipps (1992c) argues that what is required for successful learning is a high level of sustained interaction with greater use of intellectually challenging communication (higher–order statements and questioning) in a setting where children are given some responsibility for their own learning. A number of research studies indicate that approaches to teaching which rely on individual communication between teacher and child and rarely focus on the class as a whole or on groups of children can cause problems. This is because with average and above sized classes (25 to 30 or more pupils) there are very low levels of teacher interaction at the individual child level but high levels of interaction for teachers much of which is fragmented and routine. The sensitive use of whole class teaching for a proportion of teacher time where appropriate could raise the overall level of teacher–pupil communication substantially.

It is also possible that the introduction of the National Curriculum will lead to the increased use of topic approaches to ensure curriculum coverage. This is a development which may fit in well with many schools' existing curriculum planning. The excessive workload entailed in the ten subject National Curriculum and logistical problems of attempting to timetable to achieve adequate coverage for all areas have been well rehearsed and are broadly accepted even in Government circles. Sir Ron Dearing's interim report's (Dearing 1993) recommendation for a reduction in time devoted to the compulsory curriculum demonstrates an acceptance of this. He argues that:

> 'The content of, in particular, the foundation subjects should be defined in a less detailed and prescriptive manner, although the core subjects should continue to be defined in reasonable depth' (p 27).

> 'The basic aim . is to provide significantly greater scope for the exercise of professional judgement than exists at present' (p 29).

At Key Stage 2 he recommends that 15 to 20 per cent of teaching time should be available for optional work in the National Curriculum subjects or for non–national curriculum activities.

Muschamp *et al.* (1992) examined the implementation of the National Curriculum at Key Stage 1 and reported that the most common response amongst their case study schools was one of adaptation and modification of the National Curriculum. All schools in their sample actively explored cross–curricular opportunities with the aim of reducing curriculum pressure. For example, some schools attempted to identify study skills common to different subjects and decided to teach more than one subject via integrated activities or topics. It can be argued that the planned use of topics could help to provide more coherent and meaningful pupil learning activities and experiences, as well as making the teacher's task of organising curriculum delivery much more manageable (Muschamp *et al.*, 1992).

Against this, however, there may be strong pressures to downgrade the use of integrated topic–based approaches in favour of subject–based and specialist teaching as noted earlier (e.g.: recommendations by the HMI (DES 1991b, OFSTED 1993b, NCC 1993b). Such pressures may cause additional organisational difficulties for teachers in attempting to cover all the National Curriculum subjects, and reduce their ability to offer worthwhile curriculum experiences for pupils. Nonetheless, there is evidence that topic based approaches to the delivery of learning may lead to fragmentation in coverage of different subjects and can involve much routine low level activity for pupils (Alexander, 1984, 1992) unless carefully planned (in terms of learning objectives), assessed and evaluated. OFSTED's (1993b) report provides a list of factors associated with successful topic work which is relevant in this context. In particular, OFSTED suggests that topics should have a single subject bias or emphasise particular subjects and:

'whole–school agreement about subject coverage and the balance between subjects and topics, the outcomes of which are monitored by members of the senior management team' (p 21).

It is, of course, possible to envisage the use of carefully planned topic work with particular subject bias and organised in such a way that all or most pupils are working in the same curriculum area during the same session, and with an appropriate mix of whole–class group and individual teaching. Single subject and whole class approaches need not, of necessity, preclude the use of topic approaches. It is unfortunate that the old and sterile debate about 'progressive' versus 'formal' teaching styles tends to dominate considerations of teaching approaches.

Greater use of single ability grouping or streaming may be a potential consequence of the implementation of the National Curriculum at Key Stage 2, especially in the light of the NCC (1993b) proposals. Although such groupings may simplify classroom organisation, the possibility of negative consequences for some children must be addressed. Because streaming/formal ability grouping has been very little used in primary schools in recent years no up–to–date studies of its impact have been conducted. However, work by Barker Lunn (1970) and Douglas (1964) suggests that streaming can lower the self–esteem of low–attaining children. The possibility that negative early labelling of children and reduced teacher expectations for particular groups may result from the increased use of early formal assessment at Key Stage 1 needs to be balanced against the supposed benefits of the use of such organisational strategies. Moreover, reviews of aptitude–treatment interaction have indicated that ability grouping is most effective when carried out for only some subjects and for only part of the school day (Cronbach & Snow, 1977; Slavin, 1987). In addition, it should be recognised that ability grouping may also make the use of whole class approaches to teaching impractical or inappropriate.

Finally, there is strong evidence to suggest that organisational difficulties in delivering the National Curriculum are likely to be most acute in mixed–aged classes (Muschamp *et al.*, 1992) and this is an issue which requires further investigation.

PUPIL LEARNING

Research evidence suggests that the implementation of the National Curriculum at Key Stage 2 is likely to lead to a number of important changes in the way teachers approach the task of matching curriculum activities and experiences to pupils' perceived needs. This in turn would be expected to influence pupils' learning and progress.

The National Curriculum entails a greater focus on pupil assessment and on teacher and school record keeping concerning individual pupil attainment and progress. Enhanced pupil learning might be expected to result from improved assessment and record teaching practices and the attention paid to pupil progress if such assessment is used formatively/diagnostically (see Mortimore *et al.* 1988, Tizard *et al.* 1988, DES 1991c, Gipps *et al.*, 1992; Harlen *et al.* 1992). In addition, enhanced pupil learning might also be expected as a result of the more equal curriculum coverage within and between classes and schools which is one of the intended consequences of the National Curriculum. Research suggests that wide variations in curriculum coverage exist which cannot be fully explained by reference to the intake characteristics of classes/schools or variations individual pupil ability (Bennett *et al.* 1984, Tizard *et al.*, 1988). Pupils cannot be expected to learn if they do not have access to particular learning experiences and bodies of knowledge, and curriculum coverage has been shown to have an impact on children's attainment and progress (Tizard *et al.* 1988; Plewis & Veltman 1992). In addition, work by Osborn & Pollard (1991) indicates that teachers often value the National Curriculum structure and guidelines particularly in some specialist subjects about which they feel less confident of their own expertise. Enhanced pupil learning might be expected as a positive result of teachers' improved curriculum knowledge due to the availability of the National Curriculum structure and guidelines.

Increased teacher awareness of pupil needs and progress also might be anticipated as a result of the implementation of the National Curriculum. In the best possible case greater teacher confidence in matching the curriculum to individual pupil needs might occur as a result of the teacher's enhanced knowledge of pupils' current skills and level, and the curriculum covered and mastered in earlier years (e.g.: at Key Stage 1). Work by Mortimore *et al.* (1988) and Alexander (1992) has indicated that continuity and whole school approaches to planning the curriculum can be beneficial.

Evidence at Key Stage 1 suggests that English, mathematics and science receive more teaching time than other areas (Campbell 1992, Muschamp *et al.* 1992, Pollard *et al.* 1994). Despite recent recommendations to "slim down" the overall amount of teacher time devoted to the National Curriculum to allow a margin of time (ranging from 10–15% to 20–25%) for teachers to use as 'he/she sees fit in the light of local circumstances' (Dearing 1993, p 36), it is likely that these "core" subjects will continue to receive particular emphasis. Dearing (1993) explicitly notes:

> 'The central importance of the core subjects of English, mathematics and science means that the statutory core in these subjects will be larger than that of the other subjects' (p 6).

However, mastery of the core subjects, particularly the basic skills receives the greatest stress at ages 5–7 years. The increased emphasis on the core curriculum may assist children's learning in these areas (though this may be at the expense of achieving the broad, balanced curriculum advocated at the introduction of the National Curriculum). There is evidence that poor performance in the basic skill areas at age seven and eleven years is a strong predictor of later poor performance and that the gap in performance increases over time (Mabey 1985, Mortimore *et al.* 1988, Tizard *et al.* 1988, Sammons *et al.* 1993). It is possible that giving more time and emphasis to these areas early on may improve later performance. For example, Tizard *et al.* (1988) report that reading and mathematics attainments at age seven years are higher if children receive a wider "3R" curriculum at infant school.

Potential negative consequences for pupil learning include the suppression of the formative purposes of assessment by pressure to provide accurate and fair end–of–Key Stage results for summative purposes (see Harlen & Qualter, 1991), less emphasis on teacher assessment and the desire for simple pencil and paper tests (Harlen *et al.*, 1992). This could lead to poorer pupil progress and match of tasks. However, Dearing's (1993) recent report has gone a long way towards reducing such potential negative consequences by the reduction in national testing requirements and by explicit recommendation that teacher assessment and national tests be given 'equal standing in future reporting arrangements' (p 2), and proposals to enhance the status of soundly based teacher assessment and foster its development.

The recommendations of Dearing's (1993) report should also help to reduce the excessive workload of the National Curriculum which research suggests was leading to increase of stress for teachers and extreme difficulties in covering all the National Curriculum areas adequately (Campbell 1992, 1993, Alexander 1992, Osborn & Pollard 1991, Pollard 1993, Webb 1993a).

Nonetheless, difficulties remain in the delivery of the National Curriculum because of the lack of sufficient numbers of specialist teachers and teachers' lack of confidence in their abilities to deal with all subjects in the National Curriculum. These difficulties are likely to be particularly acute at Key Stage 2 (Alexander 1992, Campbell 1992; Muschamp *et al.* 1992) and have obvious consequences for the quality of pupil learning. Bennett, Summers & Askew, in this volume, provide further analysis of the issue of knowledge for teaching and teaching performance.

LANGUAGE AND LEARNING

To grasp fully the possible implications of the National Curriculum at Key Stage 2 for children's learning, it is important to consider the role of *language* in learning. This is a topic that has received a great deal of attention over the last twenty years or so, and although there are differences of approach and opinion, there is little dissent about the centrality of language in the learning process. In fact, few would disagree with the proposition that children (in common with us all)—do their learning, and their thinking, through language. This section starts by reviewing some of the major findings relating to language and learning, and then attempts to relate these to the possible futures hinted at in the National Curriculum documents.

Much of what is known about the links between language and learning derives from studies of children's spoken language development during their pre-school years—a time when all children make astonishing learning gains, entirely without experience of formal 'teaching', and long before they are able to read and write. The reasons for this learning explosion seem to lie in the nature of the communication that takes place between children and the people they live amongst. Talk between children and others—especially parents or other carers—is especially well-designed to facilitate learning. Summarising across the research literature, it seems that there are two basic conditions for learning that child–adult talk provides:

children are active participants in their own learning—exploring,
through talk, the nature and meaning of the world around them;
adults provide just the right amount of support, encouragement and
structure to help children move on in their learning, without taking
the initiative away from them.

Regarding the first point: children are *active participants* in talk, and hence in
their own learning, in a number of different respects. They play an active role
conversationally, in that it is more often the child than the adult who 'makes the
running'. A large body of research shows that children—across all social
backgrounds—initiate conversations more often than adults; they usually get to
choose, and change, the topic, and they often set the 'agenda' for talk by asking
questions, making suggestions and modifying other people's ideas and plans (e.g.:
Wells 1986, MacLure 1992, McTear 1985, Tizard & Hughes 1984). They are also
cognitively, or intellectually active, in that their talk displays the kind of 'higher
order' reasoning that is valued in our education system and strongly associated
with learning, such as hypothesising, speculating, generalising, weighing up
alternatives, seeing things from the perspectives of other people (e.g.: Tizard &
Hughes 1984)—although it has been argued that some children get less opportunity
than others to engage in this kind of 'higher order' thinking through language (e.g.:
Tough 1977, Blank 1973). Finally, children are active *theorisers* in that, through
talk, they are continuously trying to make sense of the world and the people in it,
searching for patterns and regularities, and using the 'feedback' that they get from
their conversational partners to test out and modify their hunches and hypotheses
(e.g.: Beveridge, 1982; Donaldson, 1978). This notion of 'practical theorising'
through language supports the 'constructivist' model of learning referred to
elsewhere in this paper (see also Driver, 1983; Edwards & Mercer, 1987), and
argues against models which construe learning as the passive acquisition of
predigested chunks of knowledge.

Moving to the second point above: although children play an active role in their
own learning through language, this is not to suggest that there is no role for adults.
On the contrary, much of the research into language and learning has identified a
crucial role for adults and other people close to the child, in addition to the obvious
one of giving them access to new bodies of knowledge. Bruner (e.g.: 1983) called
this role 'scaffolding', a term that has now entered the professional vocabulary of
teaching, and which describes the ways in which adults provide the security and
structure that allows children to take the next step in their learning—for instance
by asking them just the right kinds of 'what next' questions, by helping them to
clarify their decisions, or by prompting them to rethink their plans. Vygotsky's
notion of learning in the 'zone of proximal development' similarly describes the
ways in which a novice learner and a more expert partner (who does not need to
be an adult) can interact in ways that help the learner to edge just beyond the

current limits of their expertise (see for example Griffin & Cole 1984). Parents are generally very good 'scaffolders' since they know their children's intentions and desires well, and they have a rich history of shared events, meanings and feelings to draw on for talk and learning. They are 'finely tuned' (Wells, 1986) to their children's struggles to learn and to communicate. Teachers find it much harder, with many more children to support, and much less intimate knowledge of their lives and interests, and this is one source of the well-known difficulties many teachers experience in 'matching' curriculum activities to children's needs, noted elsewhere in this paper. Communication—and therefore learning—problems are even more likely to arise when there is a class or cultural 'gap' between the teacher and the child (Tizard & Hughes 1984).

The rationale for learning in small groups—currently a contentious issue in National Curriculum debates—comes in large part from work on the links between language and learning, which has suggested that children working collaboratively in peer groups can exert a kind of control and responsibility over their own learning that may be difficult for them to achieve solely through teacher-to-pupil instruction. Many studies of primary children discussing and working through joint activities have shown that they are able to support and extend one anothers' suggestions and ideas, and that in the course of doing this they are often exercising and acquiring valuable skills of problem-solving, decision-making, hypothesising, predicting, summarising—together with social skills such as cooperativeness and empathy (e.g.: Barnes & Todd 1977, Phillips 1988, Edwards & Westgate 1987). In small-group settings, under favourable conditions, and with well-targeted and well-timed teacher interventions, children can attain a degree of 'ownership' of their own learning (Chang & Wells 1988) that can be hard to match in teacher-to-child or teacher-to-class situations, where it is usually the teacher who has the biggest 'say' in what to talk about, and where there may be tacit rules about saying things clearly and concisely. In peer group talk children have the right and luxury to be tentative, exploratory and hesitant as they grope towards new ideas and concepts. However there are also a number of studies that suggest that small group work often fails to live up to the ideal (e.g.: Galton 1989, Gipps 1992c), resulting in children working on low-level or unchallenging tasks, without much collaboration with the others in their group.

One last issue relates to the links between language, learning and entitlement. One of the clearest and most incontrovertible findings of language research has been the adverse effects on children's progress at school of prejudicial attitudes towards the language or dialect of their own communities (Edwards & Furlong 1978, Edwards 1983, Heath 1983). Children who are made to feel that they way they talk is inadequate are likely to fail to thrive as learners, since they will be disenfranchised as participants in the classroom talk on which learning depends.

It is difficult to be precise about the implications of the National Curriculum at Key Stage 2, not only because the various documents are themselves provisional and in many cases internally inconsistent, but because what look like possible advantages in one respect may turn out to be disadvantages in another. One way to start to think about the issues relating to language and learning, however, may be to consider the National Curriculum proposals in light of the three main areas mentioned above; namely

(1)   the opportunities children are given to be active participants in the language, and therefore the learning of the classroom;

(2)   the nature and quality of the support teachers are likely to be encouraged/able to provide to support these learning processes;

(3)   the entitlement of all pupils as participants in the language community of the classroom.

One obvious issue of relevance is the debate about the merits of whole–class as opposed to small group teaching. As noted elsewhere, a move to more whole–class teaching might result in improvements for some children in the quality of the interactions, and hence the learning opportunities, they experience in the classroom. However if whole–class teaching should become the dominant organisational structure in primary schools, this would almost certainly work against the conditions for optimal learning since—no matter how well–designed the teacher's interventions—children's 'stake' in talk for learning would become much smaller and almost entirely out of their own control. Children with special learning needs, and less assertive children, might be at a particular disadvantage in such 'high visibility' settings. Equally, no matter how competent teachers' strategies, a predominance of whole–class teaching would not allow them to develop and use the diagnostic and supportive skills of 'scaffolding' children in their learning to the same extent as in small–group or one–on–one situations.

Moves towards a greater emphasis on content within the individual curriculum subjects, and away from processes such as investigation, problem solving and practical work would also have learning implications, since the latter are accomplished largely through the exercise of language skills.

The proposals for the revised English curriculum (DFE 1993c) have some profound implications for learning through language. One positive indication is the revision of the weightings of the attainment targets to give speaking and listening equal emphasis with reading and writing—a move which further confirms the importance given in the National Curriculum to this aspect of children's language—although it should be noted that the revised version makes less reference specifically to learning issues than its predecessor. Many of the examples of classroom activities accompanying the statements of attainment are excellent as exemplars of active and relevant uses of language which would be likely to promote children's learning. The National Curriculum could be seen as having generally positive implications for learning through language, therefore, through its endorsement of the validity of 'oracy' as well as literacy.

Other aspects of the revised order are very worrying in terms of their implications for children's prospects as learners. The increased emphasis on the development of listening skills suggests an inclination towards a more passive, fact–driven view of learning. The insistence throughout the document on the importance of clarity of diction, precision, and accuracy suggest a model of language as performance rather than a resource for learning and making meaning. Children might feel discouraged from using the exploratory and un–polished language that is often the mark of thinking and reflection.

The most contentious aspect of the proposals however, and the one with the most serious implications, is the prominence given to Standard English, and the requirement that all children should be taught to speak it right from the start. Much will depend on how the proposals, if accepted, are implemented. But if teachers encourage a climate that requires children to be constantly vigilant over the 'correctness' of their language this will, again, work against the spontaneity and provisionality of talk that is associated with learning.

There are serious implications, too, for children's entitlements as learners. Despite statements that the standard English requirement 'does not undermine the integrity of either regional accents or dialects', and that it is undertaken with the intention of enhancing children's social and professional development, there is a very strong possibility that some children will come to feel that their speech habits are stigmatised, with obvious consequences for their self–esteem and their sense of identity. Not only will these children be at a material disadvantage in the end–of–stage assessments, but their prospects as learners may be further damaged, since they may not feel free to participate in the language of the classroom on the same grounds as those more fortunate children for whom Standard English is the home dialect.

PUPILS' EXPERIENCES

The learning experience for the school pupil is affected for good or ill, by many factors. The curriculum and its content, the context within which it is taught and the way that it is delivered.

The National Curriculum was introduced in order to provide a broad and balanced, nationwide system of education that would raise educational standards. Unlike some other attempts to reform education, such as the Hadow Report (Board of Education, 1931), the relevance of the content for the child did not overly preoccupy the deliberations of the individual subject working parties. The child's motivation will, in part be affected by her perception of the value of, or how enjoyable the tasks are that fill the day.

There is a relative paucity of evidence prior to the National Curriculum on children's perspectives of the primary school curriculum. Both children and researchers tend to focus on issues of delivery rather than content, inseparable as they inevitably are, to the experience of learning. Makins (1969) reinforces the link by suggesting that the content of learning is less important to primary children than how they are taught.

Tizard *et al.* (1988) investigated seven year olds' attitudes to reading alone, reading to a teacher, writing and mathematics—in the Infant School Study. The most popular subjects were mathematics, ranked most liked by 71 per cent of the children and reading to the teacher (65%). An Australian study (Goodnow and Burns 1985) had very different findings when the whole curriculum was included. Sport and games were declared the favourites of junior school children with the core subjects of English and mathematics receiving ambivalent appreciation. Research by Mortimore *et al.* (1988) on the junior age range also demonstrated clear variations in the popularity of different curriculum activities with physical education proving consistently popular.

Whilst it is clear that pupils at different ages will respond differently, the Primary Assessment, Curriculum and Experience (PACE) project (Pollard *et al.* 1994) post National Curriculum also found that physical education was deemed by pupils to be the most enjoyable part of the school week—despite the fact that it occupied such a small proportion of the allocated teaching time. Painting and 'home-corner' play were also popular but as the children moved to the top infants (Year 2) mathematics and singing moved higher up the list of favourites. By Year 2 the least popular activities were gender specific. The girls tended to dislike construction and science, and boys declaring that writing, reading, mathematics and home-corner play were the least enjoyable.

The PACE team found that the reasons for these preferences were in part due to the context in which the activities took place. The context includes factors such as the children engaged in the activity and also the amount of choice available. Autonomy was found to be highly valued. The extent to which the activities were self-chosen did not depend exclusively on their class teachers but also on the constraints of teaching time as imposed by the statutory orders of the National Curriculum.

The PACE research project, as with Campbell and Emery's paper in this volume, provides evidence that the proportion of school time devoted to English, mathematics and science remains largely unaltered after the introduction of the National Curriculum. With the exception of mathematics at the end of Key Stage 1 these subjects were the least liked by the children for stated reasons of boredom, level of difficulty, sitting, listening and writing. The PACE researchers fear that this may always have been the case with these subjects. The reduction of choice of educational activities, undoubtedly, is the consequence of the sheer volume of the National Curriculum. The demands on teaching time are seen by the teachers to result in a less positive learning experience for the children.

The atmosphere in the classroom, the degree to which the curriculum is seen to be over prescribed, and the extent to which teachers feel pressured, leads to their expression of lower job satisfaction and feelings of conflict and confusion about their role (Broadfoot & Osborn 1988, Nias 1989). For some Key Stage 1 teachers (31% of the PACE sample of 88) the added stress was seen to threaten the warmth and closeness of relationships with their pupils (Pollard *et al.* 1994).

When the PACE children were interviewed about their relationship with their class teacher, 53 per cent were positive, 41 per cent of the responses were coded as neutral (i.e. described themselves as getting on 'OK' with the teacher or 'quite well'). Only three per cent were negative. This provides an affirmation of success that the pressures on teachers were largely concealed from their pupils.

It is interesting to note whether the National Curriculum has affected teaching styles. The PACE project found from data collected in the Summers of 1990 and 1992 that 40 per cent of the teaching time was spent in whole–class interaction of various sorts and 40 per cent in individual work and the remaining 20 per cent being used for group work. It is important to emphasise here that "whole class context" was used to describe activities such as class discussions and story time, as well as more directed sessions. In comparison with the Infant School Study (Tizard *et al.* 1988) levels of such whole class interaction were higher, group work remains low, and there is a decrease in individual work. Teacher–led situations have increased since 1988 according to the PACE study. The Tizard project found that children had direct contact with teachers for 20 per cent of the time whilst the data from the PACE project suggest that in 1990 and 1991 the contact was 43 per cent and 41 per cent respectively.

In line with other studies (e.g. Bennett & Kell 1989, Mortimore *et al.* 1988) the PACE project found that, although children were placed in groups, they did not work often collaboratively. The rationale for the grouping of children seemed unlikely to be friendship groups. The most favoured method (by 80% of the teachers) for grouping was attainment grouping, which was justified as being necessary for certain specific curriculum activities. Teachers deployed their scarce resources of time to the majority of children with average levels of ability. They then supported, to varying degrees, those pupils with lower or higher attainment levels.

Croll's (1986) observer codes of pupil activity were used for systematic recording in the PACE project. The four categories adopted were 'task engaged', 'task management', 'distracted' and 'waiting for the teacher'. Research findings from the 1970s and 1980s, using similar measures have consistently indicated that on average 60 per cent of their time in school, children are involved with their work (Galton, Simon & Croll 1980; Tizard *et al.* 1988). The PACE results are broadly in line with these earlier studies. The introduction of the National Curriculum does not appear to have had any effect on the amount of time overall children are engaged with educational activities.

The PACE team reported some interesting variations between classes. The levels of distraction were found to be twice as high in an inner–city Year 1 class compared with a Year 2 class in a relatively affluent commuter village which had a 72 per cent of observed pupil time on task engagement. Whilst it is true that the Lawnside (the village school) children were older, it was also noted that in those classes where pupil engagement was high, proportions of whole class interaction were higher. However, there was also evidence that the quality of pupil interest and experience was greater in classrooms in which a more flexible range of teaching strategies were used.

In summary, research findings do not suggest that the learning experience for children has become more positive since the introduction of the National Curriculum, but it does seem that certain prerequisites for learning are more in evidence. Teachers have generally acknowledged the benefits of the framework that the National Curriculum provides for the structure of content for planning and teaching. Although teachers express concern and dismay over their workloads and the resulting levels of stress, it would seem that this pressure has not had a perceived or damaging effect on their pupils.

Overall, the context for learning has changed since the Education Reform Act. Teacher control in classes has increased, and there is a reduction of opportunity for children to choose and pace their work. The extent to which the greater teacher control, that is needed to organise and manage classrooms in which the National Curriculum is taught, is a positive outcome is debatable. The motivation to comply with educational demands is still essential in order for learning to occur and there is:

> 'a need for teachers to have a rich resource of subject knowledge and a wide repertoire of pedagogic strategies to convert their expertise into productive pupil activity' (Pollard *et al.* 1994 p 192).

ASSESSMENT

The most controversial aspects of National Curriculum implementations has proved to be the introduction and nature of National Assessment at Key Stages. The greater recognition given to SATs in comparison with Teacher Assessments (TAs), excessive demands on teacher time and organisational abilities, the apparent downgrading of teachers' professionalism and lack of flexibility were seen to lead to increased stress and low morale (Campbell & St. J. Neill 1992, Muschamp *et al.*

1992, Gipps 1992b). These problems were acknowledged in reports by the NCC (1993b) and OFSTED (1993b) and have been further recognised in the interim report on *The National Curriculum and its Assessment* (Dearing 1993). This provides for a substantial slimming down of the national tests, and increased role and standing for teacher assessment, and greater flexibility in arrangements for pupils working at the lowest and (at Key Stage 2) the highest levels.

A national voluntary pilot is proposed for testing at Key Stage 2 in 1994 with the first compulsory assessment due in 1995. Reporting arrangements indicate that the overall level obtained for TA will be reported alongside the test level. However, it is not clear as yet exactly how TAs and SAT results will be presented equally. Major technical problems are likely to be encountered (e.g.: is it sensible to aggregate several TAs to produce an overall measure to be compared with SAT results?). This is an important issue and requires serious research if TA really are to be given equal status to SAT results.

One potential benefit originally argued for National Curriculum implementation was the prospect of increased curriculum quality as a result of the greater use and standardisation of TA. The original TGAT proposals suggested that the development of SATs and TA would provide high quality models of appropriate tasks and assessment procedures which would have a positive role in staff development (Black 1992, DES 1988). Strong doubts about national assessment being forced towards a narrow traditional model with TA being downgraded arose as a result of changes in Government policy in the first years of National Curriculum implementation (Gipps 1992b). Indeed, findings from the PACE Project (Pollard *et al.* 1994) document the enormous efforts of teachers to "mediate" the impact of National Curriculum assessment to minimise its adverse effects on pupils, and this demonstration of perceived "professionalism" compromised the standardisation of assessment practices. However, in the light of concerted pressure and the 1993 teacher boycott of SATs, the Government's position appears to have changed and Dearing's (1993) report indicates a much greater reliance on consultation and improved standing for TA.

Increased curriculum quality may also be anticipated as a result of greater recognition of the links between assessment and teaching and learning and improved and more systematic record–keeping in schools (Gipps 1992s, NCC 1991, Harlen *et al.* 1992). The provision of more and better information for, and feedback to, parents on a regular basis could be expected to lead to greater understanding of the curriculum and assessment processes and help to encourage greater parental involvement in children's learning at home and at school (Tizard *et al.* 1988, Mortimore *et al.* 1988). There is already evidence that the majority of parents favour assessment in principle (though not necessarily the recent SAT arrangements which led to this summer's boycott in schools) and want to know more about their children's attainment and progress (Desforges *et al.*, 1992). In their analysis at Key Stage 1, Desforges *et al.* (1992) also found that parents report that they are more likely to help their children with school work at home as a result of National Curriculum assessment and feedback from schools.

On the negative side, however, some adverse consequences appear to have emerged from assessment experience at Key Stage 1. Greater use of routine 'time fillers' for other children while TA/SATs take place has been noted and could lead to poorer curriculum coverage and quality of pupils' learning experiences (Campbell 1991, Muschamp *et al.* 1992). Disruption to children in mixed age classes who will be affected by the events of SATs and TA taking place in their class in successive years has been noted as a potential problem (Barlett & Peacey 1992). In addition, the neglect of children with difficulties in learning may take place while SATs and TA are in progress for other class members (Campbell & St. J. Neill 1992, Gipps 1992b), although Dearing (1993) indicates that, at Key Stage 2, there will be classroom–based assessment tasks (rather than tests) for pupils working at the lowest levels. It is not clear, as yet, what form such tasks would take and how pupils' results in such assessments would be presented. As with presenting TAs, technical problems are likely to be severe.

Negative labelling and stereotyping of some low–attaining children (especially those with learning difficulties) is anticipated as a result of early 'high stakes' assessment (the 11 plus experience described by Gipps 1992a). There is already evidence that some children (e.g.: those young for their year group and boys) tend to perform less well in primary school in reading and writing–based tasks. The emphasis on these in SATs and TA may unduly lower teachers' expectations for these groups (Mortimore *et al.* 1988, Alexander 1992). Further research is needed on the complex links between self–image and attitudes towards learning and the possible negative impact of increased awareness of failure on young children's development (Sammons & Mortimore 1989, Gipps 1992a). Ways of utilising assessment information positively to assist the matching of tasks to pupils' current abilities rather than negatively to lower expectations need to be emphasised.

It has been argued that the formative purposes of assessment may be subverted by the pressure to provide accurate and fair end–of–Key–Stage results for summative purposes (Campbell 1992, DES 1991). The Government's original plans to publish 'raw' SAT information about individual classes and schools caused considerable disquiet in schools and played a significant part in the 1993 boycott of National testing. There were fears that the publication of raw results would negatively affect teachers' morale, especially in schools in socio–economically disadvantaged areas, and fears of pressure to 'teach to the test'. However, school effectiveness research has drawn attention to the need to establish the ways in which different factors relate to pupils' attainment (e.g.: age, sex, social class, ethnic/language background, low income) at different stages of schooling and longitudinally, over time. There is now considerable acceptance of the need to take account of such relationships in any comparisons of schools' academic performance (McPherson 1992). Studies such as those by Mortimore *et al.* (1988) of junior schools, Smith & Tomlinson (1989) of secondary schools and Sammons *et al.* (1993, forthcoming) of junior and secondary schools, have demonstrated the ways that 'value–added' estimates of effectiveness can be made.

Dearing (1993) has explicitly acknowledged the need for value–added approaches to the measurement of school performance and recommended that the School Curriculum and Assessment Authority (SCAA) commission research into operational approaches to a measure of value–added for schools. He argues that this would 'make a valuable contribution to appraising performance and to improving accountability' (p 77).

RESOURCES

Primary education in the UK is relatively poorly resourced in international comparisons, especially in terms of pupil–teacher ratios (Mortimore & Blatchford 1993). The way schools are resourced has historically favoured the secondary sector, justified by the supposedly greater demands of the secondary curriculum. Under LMS the use of age–weighted pupil units as the driving force to determine allocation perpetuates this disparity (Sammons 1992). (The Education Select Committee is currently examining the issue of differential primary and secondary school resourcing.) Following the introduction of the National Curriculum the argument concerning the greater demands of the secondary curriculum can no longer be sustained and there is a need to question the ways schools are currently resourced (Mortimore & Blatchford 1993).

There is evidence that the increased demands of the National Curriculum, in conjunction with lack of resources and large class sizes, leads to increased teacher stress (Campbell 1992). Difficulties are particularly acute in smaller schools with insufficient staff to specialise in single curriculum subjects (Muschamp *et al.* 1992) but all schools are likely to be affected to some extent (DES 1988, Alexander 1992, Campbell 1992). Lack of resources may make the provision of an appropriate range of curriculum material difficult for all ages in primary school and may also mean that the necessary non–contact time for curriculum planning is not available.

It is possible that the pressures of National Curriculum implementation and the heavy assessment and teaching loads of primary teachers may lead to recognition of the need for action to use teachers' time more effectively and to provide extra support (Alexander 1992). The need to reduce work loads is explicitly noted by Dearing, 1993. Awareness of the extent to which teacher time is consumed by administrative/routine activities has been heightened by the implementation of the National Curriculum at Key Stage 1. The need for more timetabled non–contact time and for ways of reducing teachers' time on administrative/routine activities has been recognised. However, against this it must be remembered that pressures on schools' budgets under LMS may reduce schools' ability to finance improvements in staffing levels or non-contact time.

Class size may dictate the curriculum (context and style of delivery) and there is evidence that smaller classes are important especially for younger children and for those from disadvantaged backgrounds (Mortimore & Blatchford 1993). Mortimore & Blatchford argue that the benefits of a reduction in class size would be maximised by a review of teaching methods and that a British study of the long-term effects of different sizes of class on attitudes, achievement and behaviour of pupils is long overdue.

ENTITLEMENT

Two of the major benefits intended by the introduction of the National Curriculum were to raise national standards and to reduce inequalities in the curriculum experiences offered to children in state schools. The concept of the National Curriculum as an entitlement, and the need for breadth and balance were explicitly recognised.

Acceptance that the National Curriculum is an entitlement for all pupils (at state schools) throughout the period of compulsory schooling may lead to improved standards and equality of access to all groups (irrespective of age, sex, social class, ethnic background, ability). Evidence from pre-National Curriculum studies of primary schools reveals the existence of wide variations in curriculum practice both within and between schools (Richards 1982, DES 1978b, 1982, 1985b, Mortimore *et al.* 1988, Tizard *et al.* 1988, Alexander 1992, Plewis & Veltman 1992).

Linked to the concept of entitlement the National Curriculum is a modernising curriculum which 'offer the promise of real *breadth and balance*' (Campbell, 1992, p 4) in comparison with the narrow elementary curriculum which has tended to persist despite discouragement by the HMI and others. The DES circular 5/89 required that each of the core and foundation subjects should be allocated 'reasonable time for worthwhile study'.

The recent proposals by the NCC have confirmed that all National Curriculum subjects should be retained and Dearing (1993) has stated that although there is a need to slim down the National Curriculum 'it would be wrong to erode the current breadth of the National Curriculum in Key Stages 1-3. That breadth is one of the major advantages which the National Curriculum has bought' (p 28).

Standards could be improved for all children by better match between curriculum tasks set and pupil ability/skills. Evidence for the existence of poor match occurring has been found in observational studies (Bennett *et al.* 1984, Bennett

1992). Teacher expectations of able children could be raised by the use of detailed and differential levels for attainment targets. Standards could also be raised by 'teaching being planned, delivered and assessed—according to systematic programmes of study and set target right across the nine subject areas' (Campbell 1992, p 5).

Perhaps one of the most crucial questions currently facing practitioners in primary education faced with delivery of the National Curriculum remains that of the most appropriate form(s) of organisation. The difficulties arising from the limited amount individual teacher–pupil contact possible given average class sizes in primary schools and the problems associated with grouping or streaming pupils (by ability) have been noted. Whole class teaching appears to have some advantages (for maximising pupil–teaching interaction and focusing on particular curricular areas) but further consideration needs to be given to innovative and creative strategies for classroom organisation. In particular, whole class approaches may be more applicable for some curriculum activities than others. Group work may be valuable in the development of pupils' speaking skills as discussed earlier.

Children with difficulties in learning (the 18% of primary children in Warnock's definition) may be adversely affected, however, because there is evidence that the National Curriculum may be inappropriate for many children with special needs (White, 1991). This issue is discussed in more depth by Lewis (1991) and in Chapter 6 of this volume. Dearing (1993) has acknowledged concerns about the excessive content of the National Curriculum for pupils with special educational needs at all key stages but emphasises the need to ensure that such pupils benefit from the full breadth of the National Curriculum. However, exactly how primary teachers are supposed to ensure that this can be achieved is not discussed. It is important that serious attention be paid to establishing how the needs of pupils with difficulties in learning can be properly catered for without reducing teacher attention for those of average and high abilities.

In addition there are likely to be practical advantages to the introduction of a common framework for different National Curriculum subjects, especially in the core subjects of English, mathematics and science. For example, the common framework provided by the National Curriculum and assessment should benefit pupils transferring between schools and across sectors. This is likely to be particularly valuable for highly mobile groups.

However, concerns remain that the National Curriculum is too prescriptive and focused on specific subjects. It has also been argued that the National Curriculum's emphasis on cognitive objectives may reduce concerns about other aspects of the broad and balanced curriculum related to children's social and personal development (Pollard 1993). In addition, the status of objectives to be covered by cross–curricular themes remains unclear (Ross 1993).

The emphasis on core subjects (English, mathematics and science) and basic skills especially at Key Stage 1 but also in all the assessment arrangements given by Dearing (1993) may mean that other subjects are increasingly likely to be marginalised.

DISCUSSION AND CONCLUSIONS

In conducting this review of teaching and learning processes and the likely consequences of the implementation of the National Curriculum at Key Stage 2 we have been acutely conscious of the confusion and pace of change affecting the National Curriculum and its assessment during the period 1992–1993. In many ways we have been attempting to focus on a moving target which changes its form at frequent intervals.

To quote from Pollard *et al.*'s (1994) conclusions:

> 'The picture we are left with then is certainly unfinished and is perhaps rather confused. It reveals change and resistance; commitment and demoralization; decreasing autonomy but some developments in professional skills' (p 475).

As a result of their detailed study of change in English primary schools Pollard *et al.* (1994) draw attention to two major effects:

> 'Certainly there is currently a broad consensus in English primary schools on the structural benefits of having a national curriculum. It is seen as providing for progression and continuity and, with careful design, it is seen as a potential source of coherence. Organisational benefits for teacher training and supply, continuous professional development, curriculum development, parental participation, teacher accountability and national monitoring of educational standards are accepted.

> Unfortunately though, the introduction of the National Curriculum into England was seriously compromised because of the ways in which professional committed teachers were alienated. As our data have shown, the Education Reform Act brought enormous changes for teachers. However, rather than providing a legislative framework through which they could offer and fulfil their professional commitment, the reforms introduced constraint and regulation into almost every area of teachers' work. Yet it seems more unlikely that education standards can rise without the wholehearted commitment of teachers, working to support pupils' learning' (p 476).

Our review, in line with that of Webb (1993a) and Pollard *et al.* (1994), clearly demonstrates the need to reduce teacher stress and workload by a reduction in the SAT and TA requirements for the different National Curriculum subjects without sacrificing the breadth and balance of the National Curriculum. The belated recognition of this (NCC 1993b) and Dearing's (1993) proposals for reducing the excessive content and plethora of statements of attainments are to be welcomed. Nonetheless, the emphasis given to the core subjects of English, mathematics and science in Dearing's recommendations may make it hard to ensure that breadth and balance are retained. In particular we feel there is a danger that an overemphasis on cognitive objectives at the expense of concerns about children's personal and social development may ensue. To avoid this it is important that the institution of whole school policies on these aspects is encouraged.

The consequences (both intended and unintended) of the implementation of the National Curriculum for the quality of pupils' learning experiences and the crucially important topic of language and learning also need to be addressed. There is a danger that pupils will experience less autonomy and fewer opportunities to participate actively in the learning process. The stress laid on Standard English forms and on reading and writing activities may lead to a reduced emphasis on speaking activities and adversely affect the learning and self–esteem of pupils from cultural groups who use nonstandard forms.

There is also a need to examine the possibilities for the more effective use of specialist teachers at Key Stage 2 in specific areas and ways of overcoming teachers' lack of confidence and subject knowledge in particular subjects areas (e.g.: technology, science) at a school level. Work by Bennett and Carré (1993) has drawn attention to the importance of knowledge for teaching as a necessary, but not sufficient, ingredient for competent teaching performance.

The value of TA, particularly the formative purposes of TA, should be recognised as an on–going activity for providing feedback to pupils and parents, and feed forward to planning curriculum experiences for individual pupils. The BERA Task Group on Assessment has made recommendations concerning ways of improving and maintaining the role of teacher assessment in National Curriculum and, in particular, focusing on ways of fostering teacher expertise in formative assessment. Harlen *et al.* (1992) suggested that:

> 'Steps be taken to provide teachers with the training and materials so that formative assessment can be carried out with the rigour and reliability necessary for it to be effective in improving pupils' learning. These steps would enable teachers to be aware of and use techniques for: gaining access to pupils' present understandings and difficulties; advancing pupils' ideas and skills, based on the information about their present

understandings; discussing progress with pupils and involving pupils in keeping records of their learning' (p 216).

The greater status to be accorded TA in publishing schools' results advocated by Dearing (1993) is welcomed in this connection. However, it is not as yet clear how TA and SAT results can be presented equally. Major technical problems are likely to be encountered. This is an important issue and requires serious research if TAs really are to be given equal status with SAT results.

The benefits of providing feedback to parents and pupils concerning children's SAT/TA results are highlighted by the review as are the ways this can encourage greater parental involvement in their child's learning at home and at school. Nonetheless, it is important to avoid the negative early labelling of children who are low attainers in SAT/TAs and to be sensitive to the possible impact of such labelling on the self–esteem/self–image and motivation of children and on teachers' expectations.

The issue of resourcing primary education adequately in the light of the increased demands of National Curriculum and NA also needs to be addressed. There seems little justification for providing significantly lower levels of resources to primary than secondary schools in terms of age weighted pupil units now that the curriculum requirements for both sectors are more equal.

We think it crucial that value–added approaches to the presentation of schools National Curriculum assessment results be further developed. McPherson's (1992) review has highlighted the importance of this topic and Dearing's (1993) recommendation that the new School Curriculum and Assessment Authority (SCAA) commission research into this topic is to be welcomed. Reliance on "raw" results alone can be highly misleading for the purpose of comparing schools. It is necessary to take account of the impact of both prior attainment and background factors to ensure that "like is compared with like". The BERA Task Group on Assessment argued that:

'The value added by the school (that is, the progress made by the students during their time at that school) should be published alongside the test scores achieved, and the school should also publish the full range of its other achievements to put the test results in context' (Harlen *et al.* 1992, p 216).

We support this view.

Greater attention also needs to be paid to ways of using teaching time more effectively (including the use of non–teaching support staff) to reduce the routine/ administrative workload of teachers and to increase the time for teaching/learning activities (Alexander, 1992). Recent research by Mortimore *et al.* (1992) has provided some interesting examples and analysis of the innovative uses of non-teaching staff in primary and secondary schools. It is important to consider ways of encouraging maximum work–related teacher–pupil communication through the balance of whole class, group and individual instruction as appropriate (Gipps 1992c). The value of adopting a *range* of teaching strategies appropriate for different learning and curriculum activities is evident. There is a need to avoid the sterile and simplistic division of approaches into whole–class versus individual teaching, single–subject versus topic–based, and to recognise the importance of *fitness for purpose* and *flexibility* in approach.

Evidence also suggests that there is a place for utilising whole school development planning to assist in the implementation of the National Curriculum and to facilitate staff cohesion (Abbott & Croll 1991, Muschamp *et al.* 1992).

As noted earlier, there is a need to reduce the excessive workload for teachers which has resulted from the hasty implementation of the National Curriculum. It is important, however, that any changes made to the National Curriculum Orders are thoroughly thought through, involve extensive consultation, are undertaken according to a planned cycle, and ensure that the demands of individual subjects are considered in the light of the overall requirements at each key stage. Schools have been subjected to excessive change and upheaval during the last five years as a result of the simultaneous introduction of LMS and the National Curriculum and associated national assessment. A period of stability is required to enable amendments to be planned and managed more effectively and to build upon the positive achievements schools have made in implementing the National Curriculum to date.

Our review of the likely consequences of the implementation of the National Curriculum at Key Stage 2 is by no means exhaustive and much of the evidence available is indirect. Nonetheless, past research and experience at Key Stage 1 provides a number of indications of both positive and negative outcomes which might be anticipated in relation to teaching and learning processes. Those which seem to be of particular importance in relation to organisation, pupil learning, pupil experiences, language, assessment, resources and entitlement have been highlighted. Whilst some problems are undoubtedly due to the newness of the system and the inexperience of teachers, others suggest the need for substantial modifications to the detailed requirements of the National Curriculum, orders and assessment. In line with Shorrocks *et al.* (1993) we believe that only by taking *serious* account of constructive feedback can SCAA ensure that the necessary improvement and development will take place. We conclude that any review of the National Curriculum and associated assessment should seek to build on schools' and teachers' positive achievements, work with teachers as professionals and seek to foster teacher involvement and improve morale in schools.

CHAPTER SIX

THE IMPACT OF THE NATIONAL CURRICULUM ON CHILDREN WITH SPECIAL EDUCATIONAL NEEDS

Ann Lewis and Pam Sammons

INTRODUCTION

Children with special educational needs (SEN) form a substantial minority of the primary school population. The Warnock Report (DES 1978a) suggested that 20 per cent of children will have SEN at some time during their school careers. This figure, derived from standardised test and survey data, has been criticised as arbitrary and self–fulfilling but is supported by a wide range of research evidence (e.g.: Croll and Moses 1985; Mortimore *et al.* 1988, Shorrocks *et al.* 1992). Thus children with a variety of SEN form a significant group and one that may draw disproportionately on scarce educational resources. So it is pertinent to examine the effects of the implementation of the National Curriculum on these children. A curriculum established with the espoused aim of raising educational standards must address, in particular, the needs of those children who are failing in, or being failed by, the system.

We discuss four key areas (differentiation, grouping of children for teaching, assessment, and multi–professional collaboration) in the light of evidence about the implementation of the National Curriculum. However, we would emphasise that the points raised need to be considered alongside those examined in the parallel papers in this book on teaching and learning processes, whole school planning, National Curriculum policy and knowledge for teaching. We examine, before discussing the possible impact of the National Curriculum on children at Key Stage 2, the background to special needs provision in the immediate future.

BACKGROUND: EVIDENCE OF PRESSURES ON MAINSTREAM SCHOOLS REGARDING CHILDREN WITH SPECIAL EDUCATIONAL NEEDS

Our focus in this paper is on the implementation of the National Curriculum but this is influenced by wider aspects of the 1988 and 1993 Education Acts.

Integration—segregation
The 1980s saw a gradual shift away from placing children with SEN in segregated special education. Swann (1991) concluded that, based on the percentage of the

school population placed in special schools, there was a small swing of 8 per cent towards integration in English schools between 1982 and 1990. There were marked differences between SEN groups in the proportion of children placed in mainstream settings. Children with sensory impairments were, proportionately, more likely to be integrated. By comparison, children with emotional and behavioural difficulties were less likely to be integrated although there were large variations between LEAs (Swann 1988, 1989; 1991, Goacher *et al.* 1988). The special school route tends to be one way with few children transferring back to mainstream schools (Audit Commission/HMI 1992a). One needs to be cautious about interpretation of 'integration' figures (Lewis 1993) but, overall, DES data show a reversal of the non–segregation trend in recent years in the primary sector (Swann 1992). Similarly, 50 per cent of LEAs reported a disproportionate increase in special school placements, especially for primary age children in 1991. Whether this was a direct result of the introduction of the National Curriculum is open to debate.

The 1993 Act continues a broadly integrationist stance. It also requires that a child with SEN should 'engage in the activities of the school together with children who do not have special needs' (para. 161 (4)). It will be interesting to see how this is interpreted and whether it is tested in the courts.

Children with statements of SEN

The proportion of children with statements of SEN rose from 2.0 per cent in 1990 to 2.4 per cent in 1992. This proportion varied considerably between LEAs. It ranges from 0.8 per cent in one LEA to over 4 per cent in another (Wedell 1993, House of Commons 1993b). There was a steady increase in statements of SEN between 1986 and 1990 and between 1990 and 1993 the proportion of children with statements rose steeply. This rapid rise seems set to accelerate with a forecast rise of 25 per cent in numbers of pupils with statements in 1992–3 and, projecting further ahead, a forecast rise of 28 per cent in the numbers of statemented pupils 1993–7.

One explanation for this rise is the connecting of resources to a statement. Schools may obtain additional funding or other resources according to the specification in the child's statement. Also, some parents have exerted pressure on schools and LEAs to provide statements. Interestingly, formal complaints about SEN provision have increased sharply. Twenty one cases of LEA maladministration (re SEN) were reported to the ombudsman in 1993 compared with 26 cases in the previous nine years. The increase in statementing may be linked with the National Curriculum. Pressures of the National Curriculum may have drawn teachers' attention to the different needs of a wide range of pupils; teachers may have felt that those needs could not be met without additional resources (Lunt and Evans 1992).

Exclusions

There has been a rapid increase in exclusions since the implementation of the National Curriculum. One survey (Pyke 1992) reported a 20 per cent increase in exclusions between 1990–91 and 1991–92. Similarly, OFSTED (1993a) concluded that the 'rise in the exclusions rate is steady in most LEAs and dramatic in some with a noticeable increase in the number of pupils being excluded at the primary age' (para. 7). Excluded pupils do not necessarily have SEN, as conventionally defined, but a significant percentage of children excluded (12.5 per cent) had statements of SEN (DFE 1992).

Expertise on SEN

In various ways, the availability of local curricular expertise and resources related to children with SEN (especially those without statements) is being reduced (reviewed by Wedell, 1993). This is happening at the level of both the LEA and the individual school.

LEA level

The shifting LEA role from provider to monitor of SEN provision, combined with the effects of LMS, is leading to a reduction in the pool of special needs expertise centralised in the LEA (Evans 1992). Consequently teachers are losing ready access to LEA advice about, for example, curricular adaptation for children with SEN. Interestingly, Dearing (1993), in a parallel point, discussed the need for local mediation to deal with queries about the National Curriculum. His report concluded that LEAs (rather than SCAA, the new Funding Agency for Schools (FAS), or locally contracted out groups) have the immediately available capability to act as local mediators. Yet this local expertise is being lost, particularly in relation to special needs. The provisions in the 1993 Act for special schools to become grant–maintained also have implications for the pool of expertise on SEN available to mainstream teachers. Grant Maintained special schools may be unwilling to carry out, or will charge for, the range of outreach work in feeder mainstream schools which has developed over the last ten years and which has been another source of curricular advice and resources for mainstream teachers.

Mainstream teachers' loss of access to expertise about children with SEN is particularly important for the 18 per cent of children with recognised special needs but without statements. These children have no statutory protection or review of the resources needed to meet their educational needs. Baroness Warnock recently drew attention to their position:

> 'There is no doubt that the large numbers of children with special needs who do not have statements, and ought not to have them, are seriously at risk. Their parents, unlike parents of children with statements, have no

possibility of redress and, at present, no right even to information about the withdrawal of or change in the provision that is made.' (House of Lords 1993, col 1337)

These are the children who make up the vast majority of pupils with SEN in mainstream schools.

School level
The cutting of SEN posts (co–ordinators/learning support teachers) was reported in 15 per cent of LEAs in 1991 (House of Commons 1993b). This reduction in in–school SEN expertise was not being replaced by an emphasis on whole school training for SEN. School and LEA in–service training on special needs has been a low priority (House of Commons 1993b), presumably because National Curriculum focused INSET has predominated.

At both school and LEA levels the demise of SEN expertise is likely to be highlighted by the requirements of the draft Code of Practice (DFE 1993a). This refers to the role of the SEN coordinator in advising, monitoring, coordinating and reporting on the progress of children thought to have SEN. It is stated (para. II.79) that the SEN coordinator should call in 'an appropriate specialist from a support service' when assessing the child's needs. This person 'will be qualified and experienced in the particular area of the child's special educational needs'. Such intentions will require an injection of training and personnel if the Code is to be workable.

RECENT AND IMMINENT CHANGES IN SEN PROVISION

Discussion of the impact of the National Curriculum on children with SEN is necessarily speculative because of changes, not only to the National Curriculum, but also to ways in which SEN provision is defined, structured and organised. We review briefly some of these changes because they will have an impact on the curriculum for children with SEN.

Definition of what SEN provision is 'routinely provided'
SEN are defined in the 1993 Education Act as learning difficulties that call for special provision besides that routinely provided in mainstream schools (1993 Act, para. 156). If what is provided routinely does not meet the child's learning needs then a statement of SEN, specifying additional resources, will be required. The inexorable rise in numbers of statements, described earlier, combined with increasingly high levels of parental expectations of SEN provision is creating an impossible situation for the funders, the LEAs. Recognising this, the 1993 Education Act proposed a Code of Practice to clarify what SEN provision should

be made generally in mainstream schools. The Code of Practice and associated regulations, published in draft form in Autumn 1993 (DFE 1993a), are likely to lead to a tightening up of cut–off points for statements.

The draft Code of Practice proposes a five stage procedure in which the first three stages of assessment and monitoring of a child's SEN are the explicit responsibility of the class teacher and school's SEN coordinator. An extensive range of information is given as required at each stage (including curricular attainments, standardised test results, parental reports and the child's perceptions of his or her difficulties). The intention of tightening within–school procedures is laudable but schools will need time, resources and expertise if they are to meet these demands. It is only after examination of the child's SEN has moved through three school–based stages and one LEA stage that consideration of the need for a statement will be made.

School policy documents
All schools are being made more accountable for their special needs provision. All maintained schools have, under the 1993 Education Act (to come into force by September 1994) to produce an annual report containing information on special needs policy. This will include making publicly available the name and telephone number of the school's SEN coordinator (DFE 1993b). In addition, the four yearly school inspections by OFSTED will include inspection of special needs provision within the school (DFE 1993b, OFSTED 1992).

Overall planning of SEN provision
The 1993 Education Act gives LEAs a strong monitoring role for children with statements of SEN (including those in GM schools) but the LEAs do not have a concomitant general planning role. The right of the LEA to act as overall planner of SEN provision in the area was included in Lords' amendments to the 1992 Education Bill but was rejected in the House of Commons (House of Commons 1993a, House of Lords 1993). It is impossible to know now how, if at all, the FAS will work with LEAs. There is a statutory requirement for the FAS to include at least one person with SEN interests. Services for children with statements should be safe guarded through the LEAs' statutory monitoring of those children's needs and provision but services for children with SEN but without statements are likely to be vulnerable.

Tribunals
The 1993 Education Act (paras 177–181) has instigated a change in formal appeals procedures related to SEN provision. Local appeals procedures, with recourse to the Secretary of State, are being replaced by regional tribunals. These tribunals will take evidence under oath and will have considerable powers to call witnesses and to require evidence to be produced. It will be an offence not to produce requested documentation.

THE IMPACT OF THE NATIONAL CURRICULUM

Differentiation

HMI reports suggest that children with SEN have benefited from the National Curriculum, notably through greater curricular coherence, raised teacher expectations, consistency between special and mainstream practice, improved assessment and record keeping, and broader curricula (e.g.: DES 1991a, 1992). One of the strongest messages about the National Curriculum and children with SEN is of inclusivity. Teachers have repeatedly endorsed the message of the NCC (NCC 1989b, 1993c) that the National Curriculum is appropriate for all children (Dearing, 1993). This has led to determined attempts to show that all children with SEN can participate in the National Curriculum. The value of this is sometimes doubtful. For example, it is questionable if a child with profound and multiple learning difficulties, who makes a gesture towards the lavatory, is indicating an early stage of route finding and so 'working towards' Geography (AT1, SOAs 1b, 2c, and 2e). Such interpretations emphasise experience of, rather than attainment in, the National Curriculum (Norwich, 1993). Norwich has argued that any national curriculum would have had difficulties in genuinely fitting the needs of all children. Undoubtedly, the highly prescriptive and heavily assessment dominated National Curriculum for England and Wales has led to particular difficulties in sustaining the notion of this National Curriculum as, in practice, a curriculum for all.

Differentiation has been a major concern of researchers, teachers and commentators. This is illustrated by the publication of a special issue of *The British Journal of Special Education* (March, 1992) devoted entirely to analysis and discussion of the principles and practice of differentiation. This concern with differentiation has divided special educators. There is little consensus about the appropriate foci of differentiation.

Differentiation of teaching methods

Stress on the inclusivity of the National Curriculum has led to efforts to adapt the National Curriculum, without formally disapplying it, in ways that will meet the requirements of children with SEN. It has been argued that to do otherwise will lead to marginalisation of children with SEN (and their teachers), limited educational integration and greater negative stereotyping (Ashdown *et al.* 1991).

Differentiation has been seen, by many teachers working with children with SEN, in the context of differentiation of teaching method. This has generated many examples of differentiation of curricular materials for children with particular SEN (e.g.: NCC 1992a, 1992b, 1992c) and has led the NCC to propose the setting up of a catalogue of associated 'good practice' (Stevens 1993). Differentiation of teaching method has grown from a narrow interpretation, such as creating parallel worksheets, to something much broader encompassing modifications to pupil grouping, mode of response, mode of access, interest levels, and pace of learning (Lewis 1991, 1992). HMI found that teachers have, within the curricular objectives of the National Curriculum, adapted teaching methods for pupils with SEN and this has led to a better match of work (DES 1992).

The types of differentiation described so far do not require any formal modification of the National Curriculum. They operate within the, currently limited, flexibility of the National Curriculum. Differentiation can also be done through a formal modification of the National Curriculum through a child's statement of SEN (for example, specifying that only certain parts of programmes of study are included in the child's curriculum, or exempting the child from summative assessments). Clarification is needed about formal disapplication and modification of the National Curriculum. LEAs and schools are confused about the detail of this, e.g.: permissible uncoupling of age and stage, procedures and situations in which temporary disapplication may be used and for which elements of the National Curriculum. Some schools are making informal modifications to the National Curriculum that, elsewhere, would be deemed to require formal procedures. This has led to some LEA documentation for schools about the statutory position (e.g.: Wiltshire, Northamptonshire, Warwickshire) but there are gaps in this information that appear to stem from uncertainty at SEAC/DFE level. It is not clear what the repercussions would be of LEA documentation giving misinformation or misinterpreting the statutory position. The setting up of a SEN special interest group in the Education Law Association (Harris 1992) suggests that lawyers have an active interest in the area. This group may well become more important because of the setting up of tribunals, framed in a legalistic and confrontational way, to hear appeals concerning special needs provision (1993 Education Act).

Radical differentiation

Differentiation of teaching methods, described above, has been characterised as making the child fit the curriculum, rather than the curriculum fit the child. More broadly, differentiation has been applied to educational aims and goals, not only teaching method (Daniels and Ware 1990, Norwich 1990, White 1991). We term this 'radical differentiation' to distinguish it from the narrower interpretation of differentiation described above. Radical differentiation raises more fundamental questions about the nature and purposes of special, and other, education. It leads to questioning of the appropriateness of the educational objectives embodied in the National Curriculum. Proponents argue that the inappropriateness of the National Curriculum, particularly for children with SEN, is being disguised through misguided enthusiasm for inclusivity (actively encouraged by the NCC). The implication is that if the National Curriculum is recognised as being inappropriate for some children, then the foundation of the National Curriculum, that the goals of education are the same for all children, is called into question. (See O'Hear and White 1991 for discussion of an alternative national curriculum). There are many groups (including children for whom English is a second language, and the outstandingly scientific, artistic or athletic) for whom one might claim, even at primary level, atypical educational priorities.

Differentiation, flexibility and resources
Resource and curriculum issues are interdependent. This point is made explicitly by the House of Commons Select Committee:

'Demand for statements might be reduced . [by] a more sensitively differentiated delivery of the national curriculum'. (House of Commons 1993b, para. 33)

If teachers can routinely differentiate the curriculum, then there is no case for additional resources to enable a child to access the National Curriculum. If extra resources are not needed then, by definition, there is no need for the child to be given a statement of SEN. By implication, changes to the National Curriculum that make it more flexible, and so inclusive of children with SEN, should also reduce the demand for statements. The draft Code of Practice (DFE 1993a) effectively shifts the boundary line for statements by moving responsibility more squarely into the school's court.

Dearing (1993) makes reference to three ways of increasing the flexibility of the National Curriculum. First, proposals for statutory and non–statutory studies in each foundation subject would meet some concerns of those who see the existing National Curriculum as appropriate for children with SEN but too unwieldy. A division into statutory and non–statutory studies would remove the need for a particular type of differentiation, that is, a greater emphasis for some children on what are likely to become the statutory studies (e.g.: number in the mathematics curriculum) and less emphasis on what are likely to become non–statutory studies. This would enable more time (and varied resources) to be spent on mastery of the statutory studies for some children.

Second, an over rigid coupling of chronological age and National Curriculum stage/level has led to problems for those children who do not have statements of SEN that separate age and stage. For example, children who are at level 1 in Key Stage 2 fall outside the statutory range (Bartlett and Peacey 1992). This is a particularly acute problem in the mathematics orders as these programmes of study are defined by level, not key stage, and so lack flexibility. It would be sensible and logical to uncouple ages and programmes of study so that children can work on material appropriate to their developmental levels, despite the National Curriculum level or key stage to which that material is notionally tied.

Third, Dearing (1993) suggested that time allocations for the National Curriculum are not the same at different key stages. Thus there is an acknowledgement that the same general curricular emphasis is not appropriate at Key Stage 1 and 2. The basis for these differential time allocations for the National Curriculum rest on presumed teaching/learning priorities. Once that principle is accepted then one has grounds for arguing that it is valid, and so should be built into the National Curriculum, to vary time on the National Curriculum according to developmental (not just chronological) ages. Dearing (1993) proposed that the National Curriculum should take up 85–90 per cent of learning time at Key Stage 1 and 80–85 per cent at Key Stage 2. It has been proposed that the National Curriculum should occupy approximately 70 per cent of the total curriculum for children with SEN (NCC 1993b). This would leave more time for their teachers to address those children's social needs. Dearing's interim report says little about cross–curricular strategies, including personal and social education, yet these are likely to be a major part of the curriculum for some children with SEN (particularly emotional and behavioural difficulties). Unless revision to the National Curriculum includes sufficient flexibility to increase this element then there will continue to be pressure to take some groups of children with SEN out of the National Curriculum.

Grouping of children for teaching

Withdrawal groups

The National Curriculum has also had an impact on the grouping of children with SEN. HMI (DES 1990c) reported that the National Curriculum was associated with more withdrawal group work. Withdrawal group work with children with SEN has been a contentious issue for some years. There are two relevant questions: (i) is it effective and (ii) if so, are gains transferred from withdrawal to mainstream classwork? The Audit Commission/HMI Report (1992a) concluded that the quality of work in withdrawal group sessions was not notably higher than in class lessons. However, withdrawal group work has been found to be a popular strategy (with classroom teachers) for meeting SEN (Croll and Moses 1985). Research evidence has pointed to gains in withdrawal groups but a lack of transfer of these learning gains once the child returned to the mainstream class full time (Sindelar and Deno, 1978; Lavers *et al.*, 1986). HMI concluded that the National Curriculum was associated with better coordination of withdrawal with mainstream classwork (DES 1990c).

In–class organisation of teaching groups

Comparisons between the findings of Tizard *et al.* (1988) into infant school practice before the National Curriculum and the PACE project post National Curriculum (Pollard *et al.* 1994) show possible adverse effects on the grouping of children with SEN. The PACE project found higher levels of whole class interaction, lower incidence of group work and decreased individual work. Unless whole class interaction includes differentiated materials, the work, usually aimed at the middle of the class, is likely to be inappropriate for many children with SEN. So a trend towards greater whole class interaction intensifies the need for good differentiation of learning materials, discussed earlier. In addition, children with SEN who lack confidence are unlikely to contribute in whole class lessons and so will become increasingly marginalised in this type of classroom organisation.

It may be argued that these difficulties could be avoided if children were allocated to classes on the basis of similar attainment levels. This may be advantageous in making classroom organisation easier as it eases whole class teaching and increases children's time on learning tasks (Alexander *et al.* 1992). However there is also evidence that streaming can lower the self–esteem of lower attaining children (Barker–Lunn 1970).

Some schools have used National Curriculum levels as the basis for allocating children to attainment–based teaching groups within the class (Pollard *et al.* 1994) and SATs have been associated with a marked increase in similar, rather than mixed, attainment groups (Shorrocks *et al.* 1992). Extensive reviews of the links between children's attainments and classroom methods (known as aptitude–treatment–interaction) (Cronbach and Snow 1977, Slavin 1987) have concluded that grouping by attainment is most effective when carried out for only some subjects and part of the school day. The impact of the National Curriculum on classroom grouping of children with SEN is an area warranting further investigation.

The encouragement, in parts of the National Curriculum, of child–child collaboration may diminish the isolation of much traditional individualisation of work for children with SEN (Lewis 1991). However demands for child–child collaboration can place an additional burden on children who, emotionally or developmentally, find it difficult to work closely with another child (Bangs 1992).

Assessment

The National Curriculum assessment programme has caused many teachers to revise their assumptions about pupils' attainments and potential learning (Shorrocks *et al.* 1992, Dearing 1993). There is evidence that SATs results led teachers to revise upwards the learning attainments of children with SEN (Bartlett, 1991). This is an important finding, given the association between teacher expectation and pupils' attainments.

Validity of National Curriculum assessments

The National Curriculum has been associated with wider recognition of the interrelationships between assessment and teaching. These are particularly important for children who have unusual learning patterns. Dearing's (1993) statement that 'Achievement at any level needs . to be judged in the round' (para. 3.11), and the proposed equal weighting for teacher and national assessments will be generally welcomed by those working with children with SEN. Dearing's position is consistent with that embodied in the Warnock Report's requirements for the effective assessment of children with SEN (DES, 1978a). These requirements include discovering 'how a child learns and responds over a period, and not merely how he performs on a single occasion' (para. 4.30). The NCC's evidence to the House of Commons Select Committee on statements of SEN stressed the necessary breadth of assessments, 'All pupils' achievements both inside and outside the National Curriculum should be acknowledged' (House of Commons 1993b, 108). There is a need for systematic evidence about the impact of the National Curriculum assessment arrangements on children with SEN.

National Curriculum assessments are tied to the ten level scale embodied in all National Curriculum subjects. There are flaws in the operation of this ten level scale; specifically, a longer tail to attainments than was implied in the original model (Shayer 1989, Lewis 1991). Wiliam (1992) suggests that, based on pre National Curriculum mathematical research, 9 per cent of 11 year olds will fail to reach level 2, the threshold for all subjects at Key Stage 2. Thus the structure of levels in mathematics (and possibly other subjects, the comparable evidence is not available) is, by definition, creating a large group of children who will fail to reach expectations. Yet this appears to be not a failure of the children but inappropriate definition of levels and expectations.

Summative assessments

The aggregation of assessments in SATs and the characteristics of the 10 levels (in particular, the wide gap between levels 1 and 2 in some ATs) lead to an under–representation of attainments of some children with SEN at level 1. These children, while apparently still at level 1, may have made considerable progress towards level 2 (Bartlett and Peacey 1992, Miller 1992). The process of combining data to arrive at a SAT level also masks attainments, especially for children with SEN, for whom small gains and/or uneven development need to be emphasised (Bangs 1992).

There is evidence of a neglect of children with SEN while SATs are being given to other children (Shorrocks *et al.* 1992). This is part of a broader and widely reported management problem concerning the neglect of 'non–SATs children' in mixed age classes (Campbell and St. J. Neill 1992, Gipps 1992b). Children in mixed age classes have to live through the disruption of successive year groups involved in SATs (Bartlett and Peacey, 1992). Similar ability streaming would remove this problem but would be disadvantageous in other ways.

An over–reliance on pencil and paper tasks at Key Stage 2 is likely to lead to a lowering of results for children with SEN. This could affect a wider group than those deemed to have SEN according to the conventional 1981 Act criteria. Gorman *et al.* (1991) found that 20 per cent of boys and 10 per cent of girls showed a reluctance to write. The simplification of SATs with greater use at Key Stage 2 than at Key Stage 1 of whole class, pencil and paper tasks, is likely to disadvantage children with reading and/or concentration problems.

Reference was made earlier to confusion surrounding permissible modification of the National Curriculum. Similarly, the PACE project (Pollard *et al.* 1994) found that teachers went to great lengths to mediate the impact of National Curriculum assessment, thereby compromising standardisation practices. Such procedures may well involve children with SEN whom teachers may feel need particular support to 'do themselves justice'. It would be useful for subject working parties to provide explicit and fuller information on the range of support to be given and recorded concerning National Curriculum assessments. One area of concern is the pressure on resources in the modification of summative assessments for children with hearing or visual impairments. Dearing (1993) expressed concerns about nationwide expertise in this area being stretched beyond capacity when both Key Stage 2 and Key Stage 3 tests are operating.

Reporting to parents
Detailed reporting to parents in National Curriculum terms may introduce, or increase, those parents' awareness of their children's difficulties, therefore reporting needs to be handled sensitively. Some parents may have been unaware, or unaccepting, before end of Key Stage 1 assessments, of their child's relative position in the class or age group. The year 3 teachers have a vital role in helping parents to respond appropriately.

Value–added
There is a need to encourage schools to sustain progress with children with SEN. The development of good value–added systems is a priority and Dearing's emphasis on this is to be welcomed (Dearing 1993). Its importance in the special needs context was signalled strongly in the second report on SEN from the Audit Commission/HMI (1992b). Value added approaches to schools' results are likely to encourage effective schools to take and retain children with SEN, whereas raw scores may discourage schools from taking children with relatively low attainments. There is a case for considering explicit financial rewards to schools that are 'high gainers' not 'high attainers'. This has been hinted at as a possibility by the DFE.

There is considerable evidence that summer born children are doing relatively poorly on summative assessments at age 7 and even age 11 (e.g.: Mortimore *et al.* 1988, Shorrocks *et al.* 1992). There is also some evidence (Shorrocks *et al.*, 1992, but not found by Whetton *et al.* 1992) that children who had received nursery education achieved higher levels on SATS at the end of key stage 1 than did other children. There is a need to extend good nursery provision, particularly to younger and less able children.

Coordination of SEN and National Curriculum assessments
Annual reviews of statements of SEN and curricular assessments have been poorly coordinated (DES, 1991b). The National Curriculum has the potential to enhance this coordination although the evidence to date is that schools have not always made these links. The timing of the review is problematic—should it inform, or be informed by, the SAT assessments? Dearing's proposal (1993, para. 6.17 (ii)) that each school should designate an assessment coordinator would, if taken up, provide a key teacher whose role could encompass the coordination of these two sets of assessments. The traditional links between SEN and assessment would make such a role a logical development for special needs coordinators.

Multi–professional and cross–sector links
Children with SEN are often involved with a range of professionals including, for example, speech therapists, psychologists, advisory and classroom teachers. Miller (1992) argued that the National Curriculum has led to greater collaboration and consistency in approach between support services working with individual children.

Similarly, the common curricular language across different schools, sectors and phases, is leading to more opportunities for collaboration and sharing of resources and INSET (NCC 1991, DES, 1992, Lunt and Evans 1992). This is a strength of the National Curriculum and, potentially, supportive of greater integration of both children with SEN and staff working with those children. The curricular continuity embodied in the National Curriculum is thus an asset both within and across schools.

DISCUSSION AND CONCLUSIONS

Mainstream schools are finding it more difficult to provide effectively for children with SEN. Whether the implementation of the National Curriculum (and wider aspects of the 1988 Act) has caused these difficulties, or merely drawn attention to them, is open to debate.

There is likely to be increased accountability of teachers and governors concerning SEN provision and it is not clear what influence these changes in accountability will have on provision for different groups of children with SEN. The disparity (in terms of resources and rights) between children with statements of SEN and children with SEN but without statements may be heightened. However, through OFSTED and the 1993 Act, all schools will be required to give details of SEN provision, including the operation of the National Curriculum, to parents and governors.

We suggest four immediate priorities. First, there is a need to *foster SEN expertise in mainstream schools*. The reduction of special needs support services (Evans 1992), within school special needs posts (Fletcher–Campbell 1993), and SEN INSET (House of Commons 1993b) all point to a decline in the infrastructure of expertise concerning children with special needs in mainstream schools. Yet without the development and sharing of such expertise children with special needs may not receive an appropriately differentiated curriculum. This becomes even more crucial under the proposed Code of Practice (DFE, 1993a). This will require a large bank of evidence to be provided before consideration will be given to making a statement (and so providing additional resources) for the child.

There have been moves to collate and spread information about curricular differentiation for children with SEN, notably by NCC (1992c, Stevens 1993), special education journals (e.g.: Evans 1990) and informal LEA networks. Funded support for such work would increase teachers' skills, provide a forum for their ideas and raise teacher morale by recognising their professional skills.

Second, alongside dissemination of what is deemed to be 'good practice' there is a need for a clear debate about the rationale underlying the materials and, from this, *a coherent analysis of the purposes and character of special education*. Through this, teachers', parents', LEAs' and the FAS' responsibilities and rights (to provision, expertise and resources) should be clarified.

Third, the mandatory requirements concerning publicly available school policy on *SEN should be reflected in the evaluation of work with children with SEN in the appraisal of all primary teachers* (as recommended by the Audit Commission/ HMI (1992a). This would reinforce the idea that children with SEN are not a very small, clearly identifiable group, outside most mainstream teachers' concerns, but rather, that many children move in and out of having a diverse range of individual learning needs (DES 1978a).

Fourth, as recommended in the Warnock report (DES 1978a) and the report of the House of Commons Select Committee on statements of SEN (House of Commons, 1993b), there is a need to establish *'named persons' to act as independent advisors to parents in relation to children's special educational needs and associated provision*. Otherwise, the increasingly confrontational ambit of special needs decision making will favour particular groups of parents (the articulate and the forceful) at the expense of parents who may lack these qualities but whose children may have a better case. The 'named person' may be vital in keeping open the exchange between schools and parents. It is through this that children are likely to receive appropriate educational provision and pressure is brought to bear, from parents and professionals, if the necessary resources are not forthcoming.

REFERENCES

Abbott, D. & Croll, P. (1991) 'Whole–school change under ERA', Bristol: Redland Centre for Primary Education, Bristol Polytechnic, paper presented at the annual American Educational Research Association Conference, Chicago, April.

Alexander, R. J. (1984) *Primary Teaching*, London: Holt, Rinehart & Winston.

Alexander, R. J. (1992) *Policy and Practice in Primary Education*, London: Routledge

Alexander, R. J., Rose, J. and Woodhead, C. (1992) *Curriculum Organisation and Classroom Practice in Primary Schools: A Discussion Paper,* London: DES.

Association for Science Education (ASE) (1993) *The Whole Curriculum in Primary Schools: Maintaining Quality in the Teaching of Primary Science,* Hatfield: Association for Science Education.

Ashdown, R., Carpenter, B. and Bovair, K. (ed.) (1991) *The Curriculum Challenge* London: Falmer.

Audit Commission/Her Majesty's Inspectors (HMI) (1992a) *Getting in on the Act,* London: HMSO.

Audit Commission/Her Majesty's Inspectors (HMI) (1992b) *Getting the Act Together,* London: HMSO.

Ball, D. (1990) 'The mathematical understandings that prospective teachers bring to teacher education', *The Elementary School Journal,* 90, 4, 449–66.

Ball, D.L. (1991) 'Research on teaching mathematics: making subject matter knowledge part of the equation', in Brophy, J. (ed.), *Advances in Research on Teaching, Vol II. Teachers' Knowledge of Subject Matter as it Relates to their Teaching Practice.* Greenwich, Conn: JAI Press

Ball, S. J. (1990) *Poltics and Policy Making in Education: Explorations in Policy,* London: Routledge

Bangs, J. (1992) 'And reactions from special schools', *British Journal of Special Education,* 19, 3, 98–9.

Barker–Lunn, J. (1970) *Streaming in the Primary School,* Windsor: NFER.

Barker–Lunn, J. (1982) 'Junior schools and their organisational policies', *Educational Research,* 24, 4.

Barker–Lunn, J. (1984) 'Junior schoolteachers and their methods and practices', *Educational Research,* 26, 3.

Barnes, D. & Todd, F. (1977) *Communication and Learning in Small Groups,* London: Routledge and Kegan Paul.

Bartlett, D. (1991) 'SATS for some but not for all?' *British Journal of Special Education,* 18, 3, 90–2.

Bartlett, D. and Peacey, N. (1992) 'Assessments—and issues—for 1992', *British Journal of Special Education,* 19, 3, 94–7.

Bassey, M. (1977) *Nine Hundred Primary School Teachers,* Nottingham: Trent Polytechnic

Bealing, D. (1972) 'The organisation of junior school classrooms', *Educational Research,* 14, 3.

Bennett, S. N. (1976) *Teaching Styles and Pupil Progress,* London: Open Books

Bennett, S. N. (1988) 'The effective primary school teacher: the search for a theory of pedagogy', *Teacher and Teacher Education,* 4, 1, 19–30.

Bennett, S. N. (1991) *Group Work*, London: Routledge

Bennett, S. N. (1992) *Managing Learning in the Primary Classrooms*, ASPE Paper No.1, Stoke: Trentham Books

Bennett, S. N., Andreae, J., Hegarty, P. and Wade, B. (1980) *Open Plan Schools*, Windsor: NFER

Bennett, S. N., Desforges, C., Cockburn, A. and Wilkinson, B. (1984) *The Quality of Pupil Learning Experiences*, London: Lawrence Earlbaum Associates.

Bennett, S. N. and Kell, J. (1989) *A Good Start? Four Year Olds in School*, Oxford: Blackwell.

Bennett, S. N. and Dunne, E. (1992) *Managing Classroom Groups*, New York: Simon and Shuster.

Bennett, S. N., Wragg, E. C., Carré, C. G. and Carter, D. S. G. (1992) 'A longitudinal study of primary teachers' perceived competence in, and concerns about, National Curriculum implementation', *Research Papers in Education*, 7 , 1, 53–78.

Bennett, S. N. and Turner–Bisset, R. (1993) 'Case studies in learning to teach', in Bennett, S. N. and Carré, C. (ed) *Learning to Teach*, London: Routledge.

Bennett, S. N. and Carré C (1993) *Learning to Teach*, London: Routledge.

Beveridge, M. (ed.) (1982) *Children Thinking Through Language*, London: Edward Arnold.

Black, P. (1992) Do we want robots? *Education*, 180, 9, 169–170.

Black, P. (1993), 'The shifting scenery of the National Curriculum' in Simon, B. and Chitty, C. (ed.) *Education Answers Back*, London: Lawrence and Wishart.

Blank, M. (1973) *Teaching Learning in the Pre–School: A Dialogue Approach*, Columbus, Ohio: Merrill.

Board of Education (1931) *Report of the Consultative Committee on the Primary School*, (The Hadow Report) London: HMSO .

Bolam, R., McMahon, A., Pocklington, K., and Weindling, D. (1993) *Effective Management in Schools*. London: DFE/HMSO.

Borko, W., Livingston, C., McCaleb, J. and Mauro, L. (1988) 'Student teachers' planning and post–lesson reflections: patterns and implications for teacher preparation', in Calderhead, J. (ed.) *Teachers' Professional Learning*, Lewes: Falmer Press.

Broadfoot, P. and Osborn, M. (1988) 'What professional responsibility means to teachers: National contexts and professional contexts', *British Journal of Sociology of Education*, 9, 3, 265–287.

Brown, J. S., Collins, A. and Duguid, P. (1989) 'Situated cognitions and the culture of learning', *Educational Researcher*, 18, 32–42.

Brown, S. and McIntyre, D. (1992) *Making Sense of Teaching*, Buckingham: Open University Press.

Bruner, J. S. (1983) *Child's Talk*, London: Oxford University Press.

Burgess, H. (1985) 'Case study and curriculum research: Some issues for teacher researchers', in Burgess, R.G. (ed.). *Issues in Educational Research: Qualitative Methods*. Lewes: Falmer Press

Central Advisory Council for Education (CACE) (1967) *Children at the Primary Schools*, Vol.1, (The Plowden Report) London: HMSO

Campbell, R. J. (1985) *Developing the Primary School Curriculum*, London: Holt, Rinehart and Winston.

Campbell, R. J. (1989) 'The Education Reform Act: some implications for curriculum decision making in primary schools', in Preedy, M. (ed.) *Approaches to Curriculum Management*, Milton Keynes: OU Press.

Campbell, R. J. (1989), 'HMI and aspects of public policy for the primary curriculum', in Hargreaves, A. and Reynolds, D. (1989), *Education Policies: Critiques and Controversies*, Lewes: Falmer Press

Campbell, R. J. (1992) 'The National Curriculum in primary schools: A dream at conception, a nightmare at delivery', Keynote lecture given to the annual conference of the British Association for the Advancement of Science, Southampton University, August.

Campbell, R. J. (ed.) (1993) *Breadth and Balance in the Primary Curriculum*, Lewes: Falmer Press.

Campbell, R. J. and Neill, S. R. StJ., (1990) *1330 Days*, London: Assistant Masters and Mistresses Association

Campbell, R. J., Evans, L., Neill, S. R. StJ. and Packwood, S. (1991) *Workloads, Achievement and Stress*, London: Assistant Master and Mistressess Association.

Campbell, R. J. and Neill, S. R. StJ. (1992) *Teacher Time and Curriculum Manageability*, London: Assistant Master and Mistressess Association.

Campbell, R. J. and Neill, S. R. StJ. (forthcoming) *Primary Teachers at Work*, London: Routledge

Chang, G. L. & Wells, G. (1988) 'The literate potential of collaborative talk', in MacLure, M., Phillips, T., and Wilkinson, A. (ed) *Oracy Matters*, Milton Keynes: Open University Press.

Clerkin, C. (1985) 'What do primary school heads actually do all day?' *School Organisation*, 5, 4, 287–300.

Clift, P. S., Nuttall, D. L. and McCormick, R. (1987) *Studies in School Self-Evaluation*. Lewes: Falmer Press.

Coulson, A. A. (1980) 'The role of the primary head', in Bush, T. *et al.* (ed.) *Approaches to School Management*, London: Harper and Row.

Craig, I. *et al.* (1990) *Primary Headship in the 1990s*, Harlow: Longman.

Croll, P. (1986) *Systematic Observation*, London: Falmer Press.

Croll, P. and Moses, D. (1985) *One in Five*, London: Routledge and Kegan Paul.

Cronbach, L. J. and Snow, R. E. (1977) *Abilities and Instructional Methods*, New York: Irvington.

Dadds, M. (1993) 'The changing face of topic work in the primary curriculum', *The Curriculum Journal*, 4, 2, 253–267.

Daniels, H. and Ware, J. (ed) (1990) *Special Educational Needs and the National Curriculum*, Bedford Way Series, London: Kogan Page/ Institute of Education, University of London.

Dearing, R. (1993) *The National Curriculum and its Assessment: Interim Report*, York: National Curriculum Council & School Examination Assessment Council.

Department for Education (DFE) (1992a) *Reports on Individual Pupil's Achievements*, Circular 14/92

Department for Education (DFE) (1992b) *Exclusions—A discussion paper*, London: DFE.

Department for Education (DFE) (1992c) *Education Assessment Arrangements*, Circular 12/92

Department for Education (DFE) (1993a) *Draft Code of Practice* London: DFE

Department for Education (DFE) (1993b) 'Schools must spell out special needs policies', *Press release 4/93*, 7 January, London: DFE.

Department for Education (DFE) (1993c) *English for Ages 5 to 16*, London: DFE.

Department of Education and Science (DES) (1978a) *Special Educational Needs,* (The Warnock Report) London: HMSO.

Department of Education and Science (DES) (1978b) *Primary Education in England: A Survey by HMI,* London: HMSO.

Department of Education and Science (DES) (1981) *The School Curriculum,* London: HMSO.

Department of Education and Science (DES) (1982) *Education 5—9: An Illustrative Survey,* London: HMSO.

Department of Education and Science (DES) (1985a) *The Curriculum from 5—16: Curriculum Matters 2,* London: HMSO

Department of Education and Science (DES) (1985b) *Education 8—12 in Middle and Combined Schools,* London: HMSO.

Department of Education and Science (DES) (1987a) *Primary Staffing Survey,* London: HMSO

Department of Education and Science (DES) (1987b) *National Curriculum: A Consultative Document,* London: HMSO

Department of Education and Science (DES) (1988) *Task Group on Assessment and Testing: A Report,* London: HMSO.

Department of Education and Science (DES) (1989a, 1989b, 1990a) Series of reports called: *The Implementation of the National Curriculum in Primary Schools,* Summer 1989, Autumn 1989, Summer 1990

Department of Education and Science (DES) (1989c) *Circular 5/89,* London: HMSO

Department of Education and Science (DES) (1990b) *Standards in Education 1988–90: Annual Report of HM Senior Chief Inspector of Schools,* London: HMSO

Department of Education and Science (DES) (1990c) *Education Observed: Special Needs Issues, A report by HMI,* London: HMSO.

Department of Education and Science (DES) (1991a) *National Curriculum and Special Needs 1989–90, A Report by HMI,* London: HMSO.

Department of Education and Science (DES) (1991b) *The Implementation of the Curricular Requirements of ERA: An Overview by HM Inspectorate of the First Year,* London: HMSO

Department of Education and Science (DES) (1991c) *Assessment, Recording and Reporting in Special Schools, A report by HMI,* London: HMSO

Department of Education and Science (DES) (1991d) *Assessment, Recording and Reporting: A Report by HMI on the First Year, 1989–90,* London:HMSO

Department of Education and Science (DES) (1992) *Special Needs and the National Curriculum 1990–91, A Report by HMI,* London: HMSO.

Donaldson, M. (1978) *Children's Minds,* London: Fontana.

Desforges, C., Hughes, M., Holden, C., Smith, C. & Owens, C. (1992) *Parents and Assessment at Key Stage One,* School of Education, University of Exeter.

Douglas, J. W. B (1964) *The Home and the School,* London: Macgibbon and Kee

Driver, R. (1983) *The Pupil as Scientist?,* Milton Keynes: Open University Press.

Dunne, R. & Harvard, G. (1993) 'A model of teaching and its implications for mentoring', in McIntyre, D., Hagger, H. & Wilkin, M. (ed) *Mentoring*, London: Kagan Page.

Edwards, A. D. & Furlong, V. J. (1978) *The Language of Teaching*, London: Heinemann.

Edwards, A. D. & Westgate, D. P. G. (1987) *Investigating Classroom Talk*, London: Falmer.

Edwards, D. E. & Mercer, N. (1987) *Common Knowledge: The Development of Understanding in the Classroom*, London: Methuen.

Edwards, V. (1983) *Language in Multi-Cultural Classrooms*, London: Batsford.

Emery, H. *et al.* (1993) *Curriculum Management and Organisation at Key Stage 2*, Unpublished paper, Worcester College of Higher Education.

Evans, J. (1992) 'A response to the 1992 Education Bill', address to the Special Educational Consortium Forum 2, Special Educational Consortium, 8 December, London.

Evans, L. (1990) 'Small steps to success', *Special Children*, 35, 2–5.

Evetts, J. (1990) *Women in Primary Teaching*, London: Unwin Hyman.

Fletcher–Campbell, F. (with Hall, C) (1993) *LEA Support for Special Needs,* Windsor: NFER–Nelson.

Fullan, M. G. (1992) *The New Meaning of Educational Change*, London: Cassell.

Fullan, M. G. and Hargeaves, A. (1992) *What's Worth Fighting For In your School?* Buckingham: Open University Press.

Galton, M. (1989) *Teaching in the Primary School*, London: David Fulton.

Galton, M. and Simon, B. (1980) *Inside the Primary Classroom*, London: Routledge and Kegan Paul.

Galton, M, Simon, B and Croll, P. (1980) *Inside the Primary Classroom*, London: Routledge.

Gipps, C. (1988) 'The debate over standards and the uses of testing', *British Journal of Educational Studies*, XXXVI, 1, 21–37

Gipps, C. (1990) *Assessment: A Teachers' Guide to the Issues*, London: Hodder & Stoughton.

Gipps, C. (1992a) 'National Curriculum Assessment: A Research Agenda', *British Educational Research Journal*, 18, 3, 277–286.

Gipps, C. (ed.) (1992b) *Developing Assessment for the National Curriculum*, London: Kogan Page.

Gipps, C. (1992c) *What we know about Effective Primary Teaching*, London: the Tufnell Press.

Gipps, C. (ed.) (1992) *Developing Assessment for the National Curriculum*, London: Kogan Page.

Goacher, B., Evans, J., Welton, J. and Wedell, K. (1988) *Policy and Provision for Special Educational Needs,* London: Cassell.

Goddard–Spear, M. (1983) 'Sex bias in science teachers' ratings of work and pupil characteristics', Paper presented to the second GASAT Conference, Oslo, Norway.

Goodnow, J. and Burns, A. (1985) *Home and School: A Child's Eye View*, Sydney: Allen & Unwin.

Gorman, T. *et al.* (1991) *Assessment Matters: No 4. Language for Learning,* London: SEAC.

Griffin, P. & Cole, M. (1984) 'Current activity for the future: the zoped', in B. Rogoff and J. V. Wertsch (ed) *Children's Learning in the Zone of the Proximal Development*, New York: Jossey–Bass.

Grossman, P. L., Wilson, S. M. & Shulman, L. E., (1989) 'Teachers of substance: Subject matter knowledge for teaching', in Reynolds, M.C.(ed.). *Knowledge Base for the Beginning Teacher*, New York: Pergamon.

Gump, P. V. (1976) 'Operating environments in schools of open and traditional design', *School Review*, 824, 575–93

Haigh, G. (1993) 'Trapped by trivia', *Times Educational Supplement:* School Management Update, January.

Handy, C. and Aitkin, R. (1986) *Understanding Schools as Organisations*, London: Penguin Books.

Harlen, W., Gipps, C., Broadfoot, P. and Nuttall, D. (1992) 'Assessment and the Improvement of Education', *The Curriculum Journal*, 3, 3, 215–230.

Harlen, W. & Qualter, A. (1991) 'Issues in SAT development and the practice of teacher assessment', *Cambridge Journal of Education*, 21, 2, 141–152.

Hargreaves, D. (1992) 'The new professionalism', paper presented to the Fourth International Symposium 'Teachers' learning and school development', University of New England, Lismore, NSW, Australia, University of Cambridge Department of Education, mimeo.

Hargreaves, D. and Hopkins, D. (1991) *The Empowered School,* London: Cassell.

Harris, N. (1992) 'Special education and the law: further progress?—Part 1', *Journal of Child Law,* 4, 3, 104–8.

Harrison, M. and Gill, S. (1992) *Primary School Management,* Oxford: Heinemann Educational.

Heath, S. B. (1983) *Ways with Words,* Cambridge: Cambridge University Press.

Hellawell, D. (1981) 'The changing role of the head in the primary school in England', *School Organisaion,* 11, 3, 321–337.

Her Majesty's Inspectors (HMI) (1987a) *Quality in School: The Initial Training of Teachers,* London: HMSO

Her Majesty's Inspectors (HMI) (1987b) *Primary Schools: Some Aspects of Good Practice,* London: HMSO.

Her Majesty's Inspectors (HMI) (1988) *The New Teacher in School,* London: HMSO

Her Majesty's Inspectors (HMI) (1989) *The Implementation of the National Curriculum in Primary Schools: A Survey of 100 Schools,* London: DES.

Her Majesty's Inspectors (HMI) (1991) *The Professional Training of Primary School Teachers,* London: HMSO

Holly, P.J. and Southworth, G.W. (1989) *The Developing School,* Lewes: Falmer Press.

House of Commons (1986) *ESAC 3rd Report: Achievement in Primary Schools,* Vol.1, London: HMSO.

House of Commons (1993a) *Hansard.* Vol. 229, No. 219, London: HMSO.

House of Commons (1993b) *Meeting Special Educational Needs: Statements of Needs and Provision,* Third Report of the Education Committee. London: HMSO.

House of Lords (1993) *Hansard.* Vol. 546, No. 152, London: HMSO.

Inner London Education Authority (ILEA) (1988) *National Curriculum Planning,* London: ILEA.

Janes, G. and Hayes, D. (1991) 'Primary headteachers and the ERA two years on: The pace of change and its impact upon schools', *School Organisation,* 11, 2, 211–221.

Kent, G. (1989) *The Modern Primary School Headteacher,* London: Kogan Page.

Kelly, V. (1990) *The National Curriculum: A Critical Review,* London: Paul Chapman.

Kennedy, M. (1991) *An Agenda for Research on Teacher Learning.* NCRTL Special Report, Michigan State University.

Kinder, K. and Harland, J. (1991) *The Impact of INSET: The Case of Primary Science.* Slough: NFER.

Kruger, C. & Summers, M. (1989) 'An investigation of some Primary teachers' understandings of changes in materials', *School Science Review,* 71, 17–27.

Lavers, P., Pickup, M. and Thomson, M. (1986) 'Factors to consider in implementing an in-class support system', *Support for Learning,* 1, 3, 32–5.

Leinhardt, G., Putnam, R.T., Stein. M.K., & Baxter, J. (1991) 'Where Subject Knowledge Matters', in Brophy, J (ed.), *Advances in Research on Teaching, Vol II, Teachers' Knowledge of Subject Matter as it Relates to their Teaching Practice,* Greenwich, Conn: JAI Press

Lewis, A. (1991) *Primary Special Needs and the National Curriculum,* London: Routledge.

Lewis, A. (1992) 'From planning to practice', *British Journal of Special Education,* 19, 1, 24–7.

Lewis, A. (1993) 'Integration, education and rights', *British Educational Research Journal,* 19, 2, 291–302

Lunt, I. and Evans, J. (1992) *Special Educational Needs under LMS,* London: Institute of Education, University of London.

Mabey, C. (1985) *Achievement of Black Pupils: Reading Competence as a Predictor of Exam Success among Afro–Caribbean Pupils in London,* PhD thesis, University of London.

MacLure, M. (1992) 'The first five years', in K. Norman (ed.) *Thinking Voices: The Work of the National Oracy Project,* London: Hodder & Stoughton.

Major, J. (1993) Speech to the Lord Mayor's Banquet, City of London, Guildhall, November 15th.

Makins, V. (1969) 'A child's eye view of teachers', *Times Educational Supplement,* 28 September.

Mant, J. and Summers, M. (1993) 'Some primary school teachers' understanding of the Earth's place in the universe', *Research Papers in Education,* 8, 1, 101–129.

McDiarmid, G.W. (1990) 'What do prospective teachers learn in their liberal arts classes?', *Theory into Practice,* 29, 21–9.

McDiarmid, G. W., Ball, D. L. and Anderson, C. W. (1989) 'Why staying one chapter ahead doesn't really work': subject specific pedagogy, in Reynolds, M.C. (ed.) *Knowledge Base for the Beginning Teacher,* New York: Pergamon.

McPherson, A. (1992) 'Measuring added value in schools', *National Commission on Education, Briefing No 1,* February, London: National Commission on Education.

McTear, M. (1985) *Children's Conversation,* Oxford: Blackwell.

Meyer, J. W., Kamens, D. H. and Benavot, A. (1992), *School Knowledge for the Masses,* London, Falmer.

Miller, C. (1992) 'Speech, language and the new curriculum', *British Journal of Special Education,* 19, 2, 71–3.

Moore, J. (1992) 'The role of the science co–ordinator in primary schools. A survey of headteachers' views', *School Organisation,* 12, 1, 7–15.

Mortimore, P., Mortimore, J., Thomas, H., Cairns, R. and Taggart, B. (1992) *The Innovative Uses of Non–Teaching Staff in Primary and Secondary Schools Project,* final report prepared for the DFE, Institute of Education University of London.

Mortimore, P., Sammons, P., Stoll, L., Lewis, D. & Ecob, R. (1988) *School Matters: The Junior Years,* Wells: Open Books.

Mortimore, P. & Blatchford, P. (1993) 'The issue of class size', *National Commission on Education Briefing No 12*, March, London: National Commission on Education.

Mortimore, J. & Blackstone, T. (1982) *Disadvantage in Education*, London: Heinemann.

Muschamp, Y., Pollard, A. & Sharpe, R. (1992) 'Curriculum Management in Primary Schools', *The Curriculum Journal*, 3, 1, 21–39.

National Curriculum Council (NCC) (1989a) *A Framework for the Primary Curriculum*, York: NCC.

National Curriculum Council (NCC) (1989b) *A Curriculum for All*, Curriculum Guidance 2, York: NCC.

National Curriculum Council (NCC) (1991) *Report on Monitoring the Implementation of the National Curriculum Core Subjects 1989–1990*, York: NCC.

National Curriculum Council (NCC) (1992a) *Teaching Science to Pupils with Special Educational Needs*, Curriculum Guidance 10, York: NCC.

National Curriculum Council (NCC) (1992b) *The National Curriculum and Pupils With Severe Learning Difficulties*, Curriculum Guidance 9, York: NCC.

National Curriculum Council (NCC) (1992c) *The National Curriculum and pupils with Severe Learning Difficulties*, Inset Resources, York: NCC.

National Curriculum Council (NCC) (1992d) *Regional Primary Seminars: Report to Delegates*, York: NCC

National Curriculum Council (NCC) (1993a) *Planning the Curriculum at Key Stage 2*, York: NCC

National Curriculum Council (NCC) (1993b) *The National Curriculum at Key Stages 1 and 2*, Advice to the Secretary of State for Education, January, York: NCC.

National Curriculum Council (NCC) (1993c) *Special Needs and the National Curriculum: Opportunity and Challenge*, York: NCC.

National Curriculum Council (NCC) (1993d) *Pupils with special educational needs and exceptionally able pupils*, Dissemination conferences, report to participants. York: NCC.

National Foundation for Educational Research (NFER) (1991), 'An Evaluation of the 1991 National Curriculum Assessment', (unpublished report for SEAC), Slough: NFER

National Foundation for Educational Research (NFER) and Brunel University (1992) *National Curriculum Assessment at Key Stage 3, 1992 Evaluation, Teacher Assessment in Mathematics*, London: SEAC

Neale, D., Smith, D. and Johnson, V. (1990) 'Implementing conceptual change teaching', *The Elementary School Journal*, 91, 2, 109–131.

Nias, J. (1989) *Primary Teachers Talking*, London: Routledge.

Nias, J., Southworth, G. W. and Yeomans, R. (1989) *Staff Relationships in the Primary School: A Study of Organisational Cultures*, London: Cassell.

Nias, J., Southworth, G. W. and Campbell, P. (1992) *Whole School Curriculum Development in the Primary School*, London: Falmer Press.

Norwich, B. (1990) *Reappraising Special Needs Education*, London: Cassell.

Norwich, B. (1993) 'The national curriculum and special educational needs, 1979–87', in P.O'Hear and J. White (ed.) *Assessing the National Curriculum*, London: Paul Chapman.

O'Hear, P. and White, J. (1991) *A National Curriculum for All: Laying the Foundations for Success,* London: Institute for Public Policy Research.

Office for Standards in Education (OFSTED) (1992) *Framework for the Inspection of Schools,* London: DFE.

Office for Standards in Education (OFSTED) (1993a) *Education for Disaffected Pupils,* London: OFSTED.

Office for Standards in Education (OFSTED) (1993b) *Curriculum Organisation and Classroom Practice: A Follow–up Report,* London: DFE

Osborn, M. & Pollard, A. (1991) 'Anxiety and Paradox: Teachers' Initial Responses to Change under the National Curriculum', Working Paper No 4, PACE project, University of theWest of England, Bristol.

Paisey, A. and Paisey, A. (1987) *Effective Management in Primary Schools,* Oxford: Blackwell.

Patten, J. (1993), Letter to Headteachers,12th January, London: DFE.

Pfundt, H. & Duit, R. (1991) *Students' Alternative Frameworks and Science Education.* Institute for Science Education, University of Kiel, Germany.

Phillips, T. (1988) 'On a related matter: why 'successful' small–group talk depends on not keeping to the point', in M. MacLure, T. Phillips and A. Wilkinson (ed) *Oracy Matters,* Milton Keynes: Open University Press.

Plewis, I. & Veltman, M. (1992) 'Teachers' Report of Curriculum Coverage in Response to Change', paper presented at the annual conference of the British Educational Research Association, Stirling University, August.

Pollard, A. (1993) 'Balancing priorities: children and the curriculum in the nineties', in R. J. Campbell (ed.) *Breadth and Balance in the Primary Curriculum,* Lewes: Falmer Press.

Pollard, A., Broadfoot, P., Croll, P., Osborn, M. & Abbott, D. (1994) *Changing English Primary Schools: The Impact of the Education Reform Act at Key Stage One,* London: Cassell.

Price, M. and Reid, K. (1989) 'Differences between headteachers' and teachers' views on aspects of decision–making in primary schools', *Research in Education,* 39, 83–105.

Primary School Teachers and Science Project (PSTS) (1988–93) *Working Papers 1—17.* Oxford: Oxford University Department of Education Studies.

Purvis, J. R. and Dennison, W. F. (1993) 'Primary school deputy headship—Has ERA and LMS changed the job?, *Education* 3–13, 21, 2, 15–21.

Putnam, R.T., Heaton, R.M. Prawat, R.S. & Remillard, J. (1992) 'Teaching mathematics for understanding: discussing case studies of four fifth–grade teachers', *Elementary School Journal,* 93. 193–228.

Pyke, N. (1992) 'Into the exclusion zone', *Times Educational Supplement,* 26 June, 14.

Reynolds, J. and Saunders, M. (1987) 'Teacher responses to curriculum policy: Beyond the 'delivery' metaphor', in Calderhead, J. (ed.) (1987) *Exploring Teachers' Thinking,* London: Cassell.

Richards, C. (1982), 'Curriculum consistency', in Richards, C. (ed.), *New Directions in Primary Education,* Lewes: Falmer Press

Rosenholtz, S. (1989) *Teachers' Workplace: The Social Organization of Schools,* London: Longman.

Ross, A. (1993) 'The subjects that dare not speak their name', in R. J. Campbell (ed.) *Breadth and Balance in the Primary Curriculum*, Lewes: Falmer Press.

Rutter, M., Maughan, B., Mortimore, P. and Ouston, J. (1979) *Fifteen Thousand Hours*, London: Open Books.

Sammons, P. (1989) 'Measuring school effectiveness', in Reynolds, D, Creemers, Bert P M & Peters, T (ed) *School Effectiveness and Improvement*, School of Education University of Wales College Cardiff and RION Institute for Educational Research, Gronigen.

Sammons, P. (1992) 'Measuring and resourcing educational needs', *Clare Market Papers*, No 6, Centre for Educational Research, LSE.

Sammons, P., Kysel, F. & Mortimore, P. (1983) Educational Priority Indices: A New Perspective, *British Educational Research Journal*, 9,1, 27–40.

Sammons, P. & Mortimore, P. (1989) 'Pupil achievement and pupil alienation in the junior school', in J W Docking (ed.) *Education and Alienation in the Primary School*, London: Falmer.

Sammons, P., Nuttall, D. & Cuttance, P. (1993) 'Continuity of school effects: A longitudinal analysis of primary and secondary school effects on GCSE performance', paper presented to the annual conference of the ICSEI, Norrköping, Sweden, January 1993.

Sammons, P., Nuttall, D. and Cuttance, P. (forthcoming) 'Differential school effectiveness: results from a reanalysis of the ILEA's Junior School Project data', *British Educational Research Journal*.

Schools Examination and Assessment Council (SEAC) (1989) *A Guide to Teacher Assessment, Packs A, B and C*, London: SEAC.

Schools Examination and Assessment Council (SEAC) (1991) *Key Stage 1: School Assessment Folder*, London: SEAC.

Schools Examination and Assessment Council (SEAC) (1992) *Key Stage 3: School Assessment Folder*, London: SEAC.

Shayer, M. (1989) 'Can standards in schools be improved?' Address to BERA Conference, Newcastle, September.

Shorrocks, D. (1991) *The Evaluation of National Curriculum Assessment at Key Stage 1*, Leeds, School of Education

Shorrocks, D., Daniels, S., Frobisher, L., Nelson, N., Waterson, A. and Bell, J. (1992) *The Evaluation of National Curriculum Assessment Project (ENCA)*, London: SEAC.

Shorrocks, D. *et al.* (1993) *Implementing National Curriculum Assessment in the Primary School*, London: Hodder & Stoughton.

Shulman, L. S., (1986) 'Those who understand: Knowledge growth in teaching', *Educational Researcher*, 15, 4–14.

Shulman, L. S. (1987) 'Knowledge and teaching: Foundations of the new reforms', *Harvard Educational Review*, 57, 1–22.

Simons, H. (1987) *Getting to Know Schools in a Democracy: The Politics and Process of Evaluation*, Lewes: Falmer Press.

Sindelar, P. and Deno, S. L. (1978) 'The effectiveness of resource programming', *Journal of Special Education*, 12, 1, 17–28.

Slavin, R. E. (1987) 'Ability grouping and student achievement in elementary schools: a best-evidence synthesis', *Review of Educational Research* 57, 3, 293–336.

Smith, D. J. and Tomlinson, S. (1989) *The School Effect: A Study of Multi–Racial Comprehensives*, London: Policy Studies Institute.

Smith, D. and Neale, D. (1989) 'The construction of subject matter knowledge in primary science teaching', *Teacher and Teacher Education*, 5, 1, 1–20.

Southworth, G. W. (1993) 'School leadership and school development: reflections from research', *School Organisation*, 13, 1, 73–87.

Stevens, C. (1993) 'Pupils with special educational needs and exceptionally able pupils'. Keynote address to the National Curriculum Council dissemination conference, Leicester, York: NCC.

Summers, M. & Mant, J. (forthcoming) 'A survey of some primary school teachers' understanding of the Earth's place in the universe', *Educational Research*

Summers, M., Kruger, C. and Palacio, D. (1993) *Long term Impact of a New Approach to Teacher Education for Primary Science: Project Report*, Oxford: Oxford University Department of Educational Studies

Swann, W. (1988) 'Trends in special school placement to 1986: Measuring, assessing and explaining segregation', *Oxford Review of Education*, 14, 2, 139–61.

Swann, W. (1989) *Integration Statistics—LEAs Reveal Local Variations*, London, Centre for Studies on Integration in Education.

Swann, W. (1991) *Segregation Statistics, English LEAs*, London, Centre for Studies on Integration in Education.

Swann, W. (1992) *Segregation statistics, English LEAs 1988–91*, London, Centre for Studies on Integration in Education.

Thomas, N. (1985) *Improving Primary Schools: Report of the Committee on Primary Education*, (The Thomas Report), London: ILEA.

Tizard, B. & Hughes, M. (1984) *Young Children Learning*, London: Fontana.

Tizard, B., Blatchford, P. Burke, J., Farquhar, C. and Plewis, I. (1988) *Young Children at School in the Inner City*, Hove: Lawrence Erlbaum Associates.

Torrance, H. (1992) 'Research in Assessment: A Response to Caroline Gipps', *British Educational Research Journal*, 18, 343–349

Tough, J. (1977) *The Development of Meaning*, London: Allen & Unwin.

Walden, R. and Walkerdine, V. (1985) *Girls and Mathematics: From Primary to Secondary Schooling*, Bedford Way Paper No 24, London: University of London Institute of Education.

Wallace, M. (1992) 'Coping with multiple innovations: an exploratory study', *School Organisation*, 11, 2, 187–209.

Webb, R. (1993a) *Eating the Elephant Bit by Bit: The National Curriculum at Key Stage 2*, Final report of research commissioned by the Association of Teachers and Lecturers, London: ATL.

Webb, R. (1993b) 'The National Curriculum and the changing nature of topic work', *The Curriculum Journal*, 4, 2, 239–251.

Webb, R. (forthcoming) *The Changing Nature of Teachers' Roles and Responsibilities in Primary Schools*, Report commissioned by the Association of Teachers and Lecturers. London: ATL.

Wedell, K (1993) *Special Needs Education: The Next 25 Years*, National Commission on Education, Briefing No. 14., London: NCE.

Wells, G. (1986) *The Meaning Makers: Children Learning Language and Using Language to Learn*, Sevenoaks: Hodder & Stoughton.

Whetton, C., Hopkins, S., Christophers, C., Heath, M., Mason, K., Schagen, I., Sainsbury, M., Ashby, J., Clarke, J., Jones, G., Puncher, J. and Wilson, J. (1992) *National Curriculum Assessment at Key Stage 1: 1991 Evaluation*, London: SEAC.

White, J. (1991) 'The goals are the same. Are they?' *British Journal of Special Education*, 18, 1, 25–7.

Wiliam, D. (1992) 'Special needs and the distribution of attainment in the National Curriculum', *British Journal of Educational Psychology*, 62, 3, 397–403.

Winkley, D. (1983) 'An analytical view of primary school leadership', *School Organisation*, 3, 1, 15–26.

Wragg, E.C., Bennett, N. & Carré, C.G. (1989) 'Primary Teachers and the National Curriculum', *Research Papers in Education*, 4, 17–37.

APPENDIX 1

Proportions of time on basic subjects and other subjects in a range of research studies and in national curriculum policy guidance

	Percentage of Curriculum time Spent on:	
	(i) Basic Subjects	(ii) Other Subjects
a) RESEARCH		
Bassey (1977) Junior	54	46
Bennett et al (1980) Infant	53	25
Bennett et al (1980) Junior	48	39
Galton et al (1980) Junior	49*	51
DES Primary Staffing Survey (1987a) Junior	49	51
Tizard et al (1988) Infant	52**	40
Alexander (1992) Primary	52	48
Campbell & Neill (1992) KS.1	51	39
Campbell & Neill (Forthcoming) KS.2	49	45
Meyer et al (1992) Primary/Elementary	50	50
b) POLICY/GUIDANCE		
Guidance to National Curriculum Working Parties, KS1/KS2	40	60
NCC Planning the Curriculum at KS2 (1993a)	37	63

Notes

1. 'Other Subjects' are expressed either as in the research data, or if data were not given, by subtracting 'Basic Subject' percentages from 100. In the former cases, the proportions of time left for non-basics are consistently lower than in the latter cases.

   *   Re-calculated from data in Appendix 4, using 23.5 hours as the weekly total, rather than the 18 hours observed by the researchers, which showed 65% of time spent in observed lessons on English and Mathematics.

   **   Re-calculated from data in Chapter 4, Table 4.1, which shows 64% of work in classrooms observed spent on English and Mathematics, to take account of other curriculum activities.

2. This shows in Section (a) the data from a range of studies (in a format that we, not the researchers, have created to enable fairly simple comparison between the studies). We have combined data presented separately by the researchers for English and Mathematics into Column (i) Basic Subjects, and have combined all other subject time into Column (ii) Other Subjects. Notice that Basic Subjects includes only English and Mathematics, not Science, the third core subject in the national curriculum, which is allowed for in Column (ii).

APPENDIX II

Notional percentages and hours of curriculum time

Subject	%	Hrs: KS1	Hrs: KS2
Mathematics	20	20	4.7
English	20	20	4.7
Science and Technology	12.5	12.5	2.9
History	7.5 - 10	7.5 - 10	2.4 (10%)
Geography	7.5 - 10	7.5 - 10	2.4 (10%)
Art	7.5	7.5	1.4
Music	5	5	1.2
Physical Education	5	5	1.2
Religious Education	5	5	1.2
Other Teaching	5 - 10	5 - 10	1.4 (6%)
All	100	21	23.5

Adapted from *Education*, 3rd April 1992

Membership of the Task Group

Mike Askew,	*Centre for Educational Studies, Kings College London*
Neville Bennett,	*School of Education, University of Exeter*
Hilary Burgess,	*School of Education, The Open University*
Jim Campbell,	*Department of Education, University of Warwick*
Hilary Emery,	*Worcester College of Higher Education*
Ann Lewis,	*Department of Education, University of Warwick*
Maggie Maclure,	*CARE, University of East Anglia*
Andrew Pollard,	*Faculty of Education,* *University of the West of England, Bristol*
Jeni Riley,	*Institute of Education, University of London*
Pam Sammons,	*Institute of Education, University of London*
Geoff Southworth,	*Institute of Education, University of Cambridge*
Mike Summers,	*Department of Education, University of Oxford*
Rosemary Webb,	*Department of Educational Studies, University of York*